VANISHED WATERS

BY THE SAME AUTHOR

Biography :

AULD REEKIE : PORTRAIT OF A LOWLAND BOYHOOD

THE TURBULENT YEARS : A PORTRAIT OF YOUTH IN AULD REEKIE

THE GOAT-WIFE : PORTRAIT OF A VILLAGE

Travel and Topography :

THE HAUNTED ISLES : LIFE IN THE HEBRIDES

SOMEWHERE IN SCOTLAND : THE WEST HIGHLANDS IN PEN AND PICTURE

SEARCHING THE HEBRIDES WITH A CAMERA

A LAST VOYAGE TO ST. KILDA

OVER THE SEA TO SKYE

BEHOLD THE HEBRIDES!

WILD DRUMALBAIN : THE ROAD TO MEGGERNIE AND GLEN COE

SUMMER DAYS AMONG THE WESTERN ISLES

Folklore :

THE PEAT-FIRE FLAME : FOLKTALES AND TRADITIONS OF THE HIGHLANDS AND ISLANDS

Poetry :

HEBRIDEAN SEA PIECES

ETC., ETC.

The head of Loch Duich and the Five Sisters of Kintail from the Mam Ratagan road to Glenelg

VANISHED WATERS

PORTRAIT OF A HIGHLAND CHILDHOOD

by

Alasdair Alpin MacGregor

METHUEN & CO. LTD. LONDON
36 Essex Street, Strand, W.C.2

THIRD EDITION

First Published	. . .	*January*, 1942
Second Edition	. . .	*April 29th*, 1942
Third Edition	. . .	1946

PRINTED IN GREAT BRITAIN

DEDICATION

HUGH SEYMOUR WALPOLE

(1884–1941)

Here, on Earth,
June, 1941.

MY DEAR HUGH,

There lies before me, unanswered until now, a letter you sent me from Brackenburn, the last I ever received from you. "To-day is my birthday," you wrote. "I am fifty-seven. The sun is shining. . . ." That was on the thirteenth day of March, when you were still in the full flush of your quite exceptional charm, and in the prime of your brilliance. With this letter and the suggestion it contained, I went one afternoon to St. Martin's Street to see MacMillan, your publisher; and an hour or so later your friend, Lovat Dickson, despatched to Macmillan in New York, under the export licence required in war-time, the carbon copy of *Vanished Waters.*

And now you, too, have vanished.

When news of your departure came over the wireless that first Sunday in June, something of me went numb—something in me went so dead that I continued in a stupor for several days. "The death was announced this morning, at the age of fifty-seven, of Sir Hugh Walpole, the novelist, critic, *and friend of young authors. . . .*" What a lovely tribute, Hugh! *I* was one of those young authors. Not until that Sunday did I know how essential a part of my life you had become. And I am vain enough to believe that I, likewise, may have meant something to you.

I have grieved much. But perhaps, in reality, we on this plane are apt to grieve more for ourselves than for those who, like you, have travelled away beyond our immediate reach.

I recall as vividly as any experience in my life the autumn afternoon we sat long over tea and toast by your fire at 90, Piccadilly, and you so enchanted me with conversation that I scarce could bring myself to realise I ever had to leave. Do you remember my reluctance to depart, and how you repeatedly tipped me back into my armchair each time I rose and announced: "This time I'm *really* going!"?

Louise, you know, was looking forward to your visiting us at the cottage among the Downlands, the week after you slipped away from us all, so silently, so irrevocably. She had been getting the place ready, adorning your room with pretty things. And, yet, she had spoken more than once of a presentiment of your premature departure, and assures me that you yourself had a similar premonition.

Somehow, your visit was not to be.

Recently I was much comforted by someone who told me that before long you would endeavour to get into touch with me again. Perhaps, you will.

You must have been aware that you were born with the faculty for getting on easily with your fellow-men. You were, indeed, a charmer, an enchanter, diffusing a broad humanity.

When I reflect on your passing—and you so full of the joy of life—I see a sprinkling of rose petals, newly fallen from a bowl upon a polished table, in a hushed and almost darkened room. They are velvety to the touch, fresh and fragrant as in the noonday of their loveliness.

Yours ever,

ALASDAIR

"Without dreams and phantoms,
men cannot exist."

OLIVE SCHREINER

PREFACE

WAS it not R.L.S. who prefaced the first edition of his *Inland Voyage* with the observation that a Preface is more than an author can resist, since it is the reward for his labours? As with the architect who, once the foundation-stone is laid, appears with his plans, and for a brief space vainly displays himself for public gaze, so also with the writer when he comes to his Preface. He may never have anything of import to say. Nevertheless, " he must show himself for a moment in the portico, hat in hand, and with an urban demeanour."

And that is precisely the position in which I feel myself at this moment.

I would be happy to have you regard *Vanished Waters: Portrait of a Highland Childhood* as a companion volume to *The Goat-Wife: Portrait of a Village*, and as the second instalment of a Trilogy. Should *Vanished Waters* and the proposed sequel enjoy anything like the reception accorded to *The Goat-Wife*, this experiment in family biography—this MacGregor Saga, shall we say?—may even extend to a fourth volume.

I return thanks to Miss Rhoda Spence of the *S.M.T. Magazine* for the photograph of 'The Street' at Applecross, and to Dr. Alick Cockburn, Edinburgh, for restful and reminiscent days.

With a few exceptions, the illustrations are from my own photographs.

ALASDAIR ALPIN MACGREGOR

Ashford Old House,
Fordingbridge, Hants.
September, 1941.

CONTENTS

ILLUSTRATIONS

EVENTIDE

The dark clouds are all gathered nigh,
And have pulled down their blinds in the sky:
Hushed is the drone of the mill,
And the sighing of pines on the hill.

I dream of the friends I have known,
Who caressed me; but now they are flown——
Dear ones, whose voices were mild,
And who loved me when I was a child.

ALASDAIR ALPIN MACGREGOR

CHAPTER I

APPLECROSS

A Sheaf of Childhood Memories

A HOUSE, white-washed and well-found, built to withstand the storms of the Western Highlands, perched on a low cliff overhanging the sea that ceaselessly laved the rocks at the foot of our garden, and that in time of tempest sent spume and spindrift to our very window-sills. Below, and running more or less north and south, lay the tideway known as the Inner Sound, separating us from Rona and Raasay and the Misty Isle of Skye—intervening, as it were, between us and *Tir-nan-Og*, Land of Youth—of Heart's Desire. Beyond Rona and Raasay towered the Storr, Ben Edra, and the Quirang, loftiest and most imposing of the eyried crags of Trotternish, in northern Skye. And away in the south-west corner of our horizon, far beyond the Crowlin Isles, stretched the serrated range of the Coolins, ever changing in nuance, and illumined at starlight in hues of lemon and emerald and amethyst, as though the Little Folk of Celtic Faeryland were tripping about them with elfin candle-flame.

Such is the earliest picture of my recollection: such was the setting of my infancy at Applecross, on the seaboard of Wester Ross.

My father was now fifty-two years of age or thereby, a man in his prime, with an exceptional career behind him. He had just retired from the Indian Medical Service with the rank of colonel. "Toward the close of the nineteenth century," to quote but a sentence from his obituary notice in *The Times* in 1932, "he was reputed to be the most skilful surgeon in India, and the most daring of solitary travellers." But for the misfortune of his having fallen in love with my young and beautiful mother (a misfortune for her and for everyone concerned), and for the obsession that he was now going to set the Thames on fire with Gaelic poetry, he would have returned to India to become, within the matter of a few months, Director-General of Medical Services, with the rank of Major-General.

Whatever else his career may have lacked, it certainly wanted neither variety nor excitement. Mainly on government service, but not infrequently from love of adventure, he had travelled round the world three or four times when many a journey now accomplished in comparative ease and comfort in a few days, or even in a few hours, involved adventure, and often prolonged danger and privation. He had cut his way through the tropical forests of Burma and of the Orinoco. He had attained the summit of some of the world's loftiest peaks, including Popocatepetl. Impelled by curiosity and a singular strain of fearlessness, he had ascended to the rim of belching volcanoes; had survived blizzards in the northern wastes of Siberia, earthquakes in the Far East, typhoons in the China sea, and sand-storms in the deserts of Arabia and Mongolia; had trekked across swamps in the interior of Asia, and trudged through Himalayan snowstorms to witness the sun rise and set. In the Atlantic and Pacific he had suffered shipwreck. He had explored the dark caverns of Australasia, and had penetrated on foot, unaccompanied, the wildest parts of Borneo and of Indo-China.

At a critical time when war was pending between France and Siam, he made a trying and dangerous journey through much of the interior of Asia, accompanied only by a native servant, reaching the Great Mekong River and, eventually, the China Sea, passing through regions never before visited by Europeans. And during the Afghan War he accomplished a forced cross-country ride through mountainous territory from Sibi, in Scinde, to Thull-Chotiali, in Baluchistan, and was then the first European to cross over the Zembar Pass, alone, though a reconnoitring party, suitably armed, had succeeded in doing so once before—commanded, as it so happened, by his kinsman, General Sir Charles MacGregor. "Picking up at Gamboli, at the foot of the Pass, a native who was prevailed upon to guide him" (so runs an official account of this escapade), "he attempted this journey as a shorter route to his destination. But the country was so disturbed at the time that the guide eventually took fright and deserted him. He consequently lost his way, but later succeeded in reaching a British outpost with a single trooper of the Scinde Horse as his only escort from Gamboli."

It was one of the Colonel's boasts that you could enumerate on the fingers of one hand all the countries in the world in which he had not set foot at one time or another. In the midst of all these travels and adventures, he had found time to occupy positions as diverse as Governor of Aden, Professor of Materia Medica at Bombay, and Bard of the Clan Gregor.

All this has some bearing on the texture of this book, as you well may imagine. The determination and vigour of a man like my father were bound to have influenced me. Of the other ingredients in his remarkable make-up you will learn something as this narrative develops.

* * * * *

The contentment that sometimes comes with retirement and with quiet reflection on past achievement urged the Colonel to seek out a spot removed from the bustle and confusion of the larger world, where he might enjoy a few undisturbed years in the throes of Gaelic poesy among a people exclusively Gaelic-speaking. And this explains how my infant days were spent at Applecross.

The country about Applecross is of the wildest, though the name suggests something of sunshine and blossom—something, perhaps, of the mellowness of the cider orchards of Devon and Somerset. Thomas Pennant referred to it as " most uncommonly mountainous ". Certainly, its immediate hinterland is as lofty, as desolate and sterile, as any region of our British Isles. But the low-lying fringe encircling Applecross Bay is, for the most part, sheltered and fertile. Fruits more appropriate to southern climes ripen on the mossy walls of the garden once trod by the MacKenzies of Seaforth when, in olden times, Applecross formed part of Seaforth's Country.

Some there are who say that Applecross is a corruption of Abercrossan, denoting the place at which the Crossan stream meets the sea. The natives never bother with matters philological, however. They speak of Applecross in their own plaintive tongue as *A' Chomaraich*, signifying the Sanctuary, with which they associate the godly Saint Maelrubha. Here, in the early days of Christianity, Maelrubha and his monks were wont to ferry the Inner Sound. Here the pursued sought girth—sought asylum—from the wrath of men.

Traditions of Maelrubha still flourish at Applecross. The memory of the Saint survives in local place-names. Although the lochan behind the old meal mill at the Milton of Applecross is referred to in times more modern as *Loch a' Mhuilinn*, Loch of the Mill, the older inhabitants, clinging with affection to the ancient traditions of Maelrubha—to the traditions of *An t-Sagart Ruadh*, the Red Priest—prefer to have it remembered as Loch Maree, a name we associate more readily with Gairloch, whither Maelrubha is said to have travelled after he had established his cell and place of worship at Applecross.

Many of the earliest impressions of my life are centred round the loch at Milton. Its water-lilies, their creamy-white cups fashioned like alabaster, their russet-green leaves lying placidly on the surface of water so mysterious in shadow and reflection, enchanted me as a child of three, impelling me even at that age to enquire into the nature and purpose of God.

There certainly lingers in Applecross something of the

spell of Maelrubha, the Red Priest. Men travelling to war from this Gaelic countryside, or voyaging overseas as emigrants, have been known to visit his grave in the lichened kirkyard by the shore, in secret yearning and under cover of dark, so that they might take away with them, and carry somewhere in their apparel wheresoever they might go, a handful of consecrated mother-earth.

* * * * *

To people unfamiliar with really wild country, the remoteness of Applecross cannot be imagined. The railway comes no nearer than Kyle of Lochalsh, or, as it was in those days, no nearer than Stromeferry, at least a dozen miles away, in terms of crow-flight, over mountain and fiord. But in the early hours of every lawful day, weather permitting, and again in the afternoon, the mail-steamer plying between the mainland of Ross and the Outer Hebrides cruises offshore in Applecross Bay for a few moments, while a ponderous ferryboat is rowed out to meet her. Even in these times, when petrol has achieved such ubiquity, this parish by the western sea is often isolated for weeks on end. Apart from such communication as may be maintained by sea, it is reached by one of the highest and most formidable roads in Great Britain—the mountain-road rising from the shores of Loch Kishorn, at Tornapress, to an altitude of well over two thousand feet, and traversing the defile known as the *Bealach nam Bò*, or Pass of the Kine. Though in recent years the surface of this highway has been improved somewhat, in order to meet the requirements of increased motor traffic, some indication of its altitude and corresponding steepness may be conveyed by my telling you that, at the present day, this Pass, curving recklessly among crag and torrent, is used for motor reliability tests. Assuredly, it would try the efficiency of any engine or, for that matter, of any driver. In the days of my childhood, of course, motor vehicles were totally unknown in this wild region; and, in any event, it is only within comparatively recent years that the motor-car has been perfected sufficiently to bring Applecross within its reach. Communication between Applecross and the outer world was accomplished on foot or on horseback, or in a horse-drawn vehicle of one kind or another, by way of the *Bealach*.

To all intents and purposes, then, my father had found in Applecross the seclusion he desired. Here he brought Mabel, my young and very beautiful and very sad mother.

And such was the incomparable setting of my early life.

Unlike the good Bernard of Clairvaux who, we are told, could walk all day long by the Lake of Geneva without noticing it, environment has always meant a great deal to me. My first memories are of my surroundings rather than my own existence. It is only in reflection that I am able to fit my tiny self into the background of childhood.

* * * * *

When recollections of Applecross come crowding in upon me, I always recall those words of Olive Schreiner that touched me with a curious poignancy the first time I came upon them. "Remembrance of delight in the feel and smell of the first orange we ever saw; of sorrow which makes us put up our lip, and cry hard, when one morning we run out to catch the dewdrops, and they melt and wet our little fingers."

So many of the experiences of childhood seem to retain their contours and colours all through our lives, though at times they would appear to get a little dimmed—a little overlaid by the newer conceptions of adolescence—a little snowed under, as it were, by the more piquant experiences of later years. Yet, I suppose that most of us, in such quiet and detached interludes as modern communal life allows, are capable of re-capturing these moments with something of their original vividness, and possibly of re-living them. We remember the first time we were big enough to stand at the windowsill, and look out on a land wreathed in snow; the first-bird song we heard;

" It is reached by one of the highest and most formidable mountain-roads in Great Britain "

The *Bealach* from Carn Breac, with a glimpse of Loch Kishorn

‘ The Street ’ at Applecross, where lived most of the inhabitants of this remote place

the first spoor of nimble-footed creature we beheld in sand or snow, or in soft earth in the garden—perhaps, the tiny footprints of a mole; the first time we cried aloud in glee at the waves breaking in yeasty curves as close to our feet as we dared allow them; the first occasion on which we were permitted to graduate above the more baby foods, and sit at table with grown-ups; the first time we gazed, enrapt, at those lovely, blue, speckled things lying at the bottom of a thrush's nest, and listened to her notes of annoyance as she flitted from branch to branch about us; the first time we recognised the significance of lamp-light, of star-light, of fire-glow; the first proud peacock we ever saw; the first gurgling of rain in rhone and gutter, that seemed a curious and pleasing sound; the first ice we ever slid upon, and heard crackle ominously underfoot; the first cluster of snow-drops on the lawn, as the snows of winter began to melt away into a nothingness that rather puzzled us.

I recall the exultant splash I made in the oval bath-tub placed on the nursery floor at Applecross, and the joy derived from squeezing the sponge over the side when I thought no one was looking. And how I screamed, not with fear but with ecstasy, as the Colonel led me by the hand among the dulsen boulders of Applecross Bay, and the tide came swirling in between my infant toes.

I well remember pressing my face to the window-pane while driven rain or hail battered against the other side of it, or snowflakes fell so thickly on it as to obscure all too soon my view of the first white world at which I had ever gazed. To this day I can visualise my idly breathing on the pane, and all the weird circles and patterns I scribbled on the misty glass. In the room containing this same window I began my first mumbling of the grace before and after meals, never quite understanding what it meant, never able to discover, when the crucial moment arrived, whether to say " for what we are *about* to receive," or " for what we *have* received ".

It was at Applecross I plucked the first flowers of my

life—the first spray of blossom, the first bunch of primroses in the woodland fringing the shore-road linking Milton with 'The Street', where lived most of the inhabitants of this remote place. Even now I can smell the first pansies the sad and beautiful Mabel picked in our garden, set down between doorstep and sea. As a child I caressed and smelt those flowers, until their perfume turned my pleasure into something closely resembling pain. All my life I have felt this pain in flower-scent.

And it was at Applecross, moreover, I became conscious that life embraced mental anguish and physical distress, as well as the abounding happiness of innocence and ignorance.

One summery day, as Sister Jessie and I were wandering about 'The Street', we lingered by a cluster of briar roses. Those little things, so white at heart, so pink at edge, pleased us more than did the big, drooping roses our mother tended so meticulously in her garden. We had no desire to pluck them. It was sufficient for us that we could visit them when we wished, to revel in their primitive loveliness. Day after day, we made an excursion to them, hand in hand. And sometimes, in attempting to count them, we tried to teach ourselves how to count. But they were far too numerous for us. Our counting capacity in those days did not carry us beyond twelve or, perhaps, twenty.

I often think of the joy those briar roses gave us both. And I was reminded of them the other day when, accidentally, I came upon that exquisite fragment, *The Little White Rose*, written by my friend, Hugh MacDiarmid:

The Rose of all the world is not for me.
I want, for my part,
Only the little white rose of Scotland,
That smells sharp and sweet—and breaks the heart.

* * * * *

At Applecross during our northern summer there was scarcely any darkness, with the result that we rose by daylight, and retired for the night when, for all practical purposes, it was still daylight. In winter-time the converse was true. Winter brought us long, dark nights, and correspondingly short, dark days. Always before tea-time in November the lamps and candles were lit throughout the house, and the blinds and curtains drawn tightly to ward off fog and darkness and the spooky terrors of the night. Lighting by ' the electric ', as the country folks call it, was still very much a novelty in the North, even in our small towns, where the gas-bracket and incandescent burner are still dying hard. But, although our lighting arrangements were somewhat primitive and limited, they served their purpose admirably. We seemed to get on so well without the so-called blessings of civilization. There was no mad rushing hither and thither. People had an aptitude for leisure in the true sense. There were no trains to catch, and therefore none to lose. Only when the mail-boat swung into the bay in the early hours of the morning, and again in the afternoon, was the tempo of our community quickened a little. Even then, apart from the two ferrymen, few were directly affected.

* * * * *

Moonlight over our western sea and starlight over the Coolins turned Applecross into faeryland. The lights of a ship or two, seen from our windows at night-time, emphasised this impression. And this reminds me that at Applecross three beings, more elusive than those with whom I had come in contact hitherto, occupied my thoughts a good deal. One was Echo: another was the Man in the Moon: the third was the Devil.

In those days I verily believed that the moon was inhabited by a huge specimen of mankind, who always smiled and never frowned. On cold, blustering nights I felt so sorry for him, living alone away up there!

As for Echo—*MacTalla*, as the Gaelic folks call him—I often wondered what strange manner of person this was, who never failed to answer my calls, and even whined in reply when I whined to him, as though he were mimicking me. For hours I would stand on the edge of the cliff overhanging the tides, at the foot of our garden, singing out to Rona and Raasay and the Misty Isle, and then listening intently for a second or so, until Echo answered me back from the corries of the hills encircling the bay. Never could I understand why Echo insisted on remaining invisible, staying up there among the hills, night and day, winter and summer, coming down not even for food. Yet, whenever I spoke to him, he replied in tones that betrayed no indication of hunger or loneliness. What he wore, and who mended his clothes, also puzzled me, since apparently no one in Applecross had ever set eyes upon him.

Echo and I had many a conversation; and I dreaded the coming of the day when we might be separated. On realising that my parents contemplated flitting to the eastern seaboard of Ross, I deaved them with my enquiry as to whether it would not be possible for Echo to accompany us. Shall I ever forget my disappointment on finding that, for some reason inexplicable in my tender years, my unseen companion could not leave his haunts among the high corries of Applecross? I strove hard to console myself with the hope that maybe, another *Mac-Talla* might answer me back from the hills around our new home. But there was no *MacTalla* at High Wind; and I soon began to pine for the West again.

That Echo had not followed us seemed very queer to me; and I felt there must have been an explanation for this, which I was not being told. After all, the Man in the Moon had not deserted us. On the contrary, he was taking the trouble to come all the way from Applecross to look us up occasionally. (Was it not a fellow from the Isles, very much like myself, who expressed great surprise at seeing the moon away in the south of England? "*A' ghealach an so cuideachd!*" he exclaimed: "the moon here too!")

And what of the Devil, the third person of extraordinarily elusive qualities, whose existence, nevertheless, was very real to me?

Our house, I already have mentioned, lay in that part of Applecross known as Milton. At Milton, as one might have expected, stood the meal mill of the parish, driven by a water-wheel, the lade to which ran from the lochan near by. Indeed, the actual wheel was not more than a dozen yards or so from our back door.

There was always great fear among the natives lest my insistence in playing about the mill, especially when the big water-wheel was in motion, might result in my being drowned, or in my falling down into its dark, dungeon-like interior. With a view to keeping me out of mischief and danger, therefore, it was agreed between our household and Mr Matheson, the miller, that they would have to convince me that the mill was the habitat of the bogieman—of the One-we-need-not-mention, the Son of Yon One, as the Gaels call him—who assuredly would catch me if I persisted in playing anywhere near it, particularly when it was working. For some time I believed all I had been told about the bogieman. Did not the dark, hidden works within often give a queer rumbling that, for all the world, sounded like his grunts and groans?

But the lure of that wheel, with the water tumbling over it in sunlight, was too great an attraction. Gradually I began to question the existence of this monster, with the result that Mr Matheson and our maids had to conspire to find a character more fearsome. To what should they now turn but to the Scriptures? I was warned hereafter to eschew the mill because it was haunted by the wiliest of all the evil spirits in the world—the Black Devil Himself!! In proof of this, I was led to a certain spot, and made to peer down some eight or ten feet at a small, black speck in the very bowels of the mill. That black speck was definite proof that the Devil resided in the meal mill at the Milton of Applecross.

It was some considerable time before I realised that a

dog had responded here to one of nature's baser calls. Hence the black speck that, in order to keep me away from the mill, had been fathered on the Devil! The only alternative was to convince me that the mill-wheel itself, which was engaging my interest more than ever before, was in reality a demon metamorphosed. But this endeavour to deceive proved even less successful. I now came to the conclusion that the sole evil genius against whom I had to contend was none other than the miller. With him originated all these fables.

Mr Matheson was the local butcher as well as the miller. He was nicknamed the Dupple, because of the difficulty he had had at school in pronouncing the letter, w. The older inhabitants of Applecross still recite the following conversation said to have passed between Mr Matheson and me, when I was about four years old:

"You are Mr Matheson, aren't you?" said I.

"I am," replied the miller.

"And you are the miller too, aren't you?"

"I am that."

"And you are the butcher?"

"Yes, I am also the butcher."

"And you are the Dupple?"

No reply! Undaunted, I proceeded: "Well, if you say you are all these things, and everyone else says you're the Dupple, *I* say you're the Black Devil!"

With this I fled to the boulders beside the loch, and remained there in hiding for half a day.

* * * * *

It was during my sojourn at Applecross that I developed the passion for the sea that has characterised all my father's people. Applecross fostered in me a strange love for the sea's edge and an insatiable longing for the sea which have followed me all through life, compelling my return from time to time to the world of wave and tide, of oar and sail, if only for brief respite. Incidentally, I was christened Alasdair after one of five uncles, four of whom lost their lives at sea in different parts of the globe.

The story of Alasdair's fate was never related to any of us by our father. He may have regarded it as too gruesome for the ears of his children. But my Hebridean relatives often remind me of what befell Alasdair MacGregor. His ship, a sailing vessel that had made many a fast passage between this country and South America, and was manned for the most part by seamen from Lewis, stood stormbound off Cape Horn. Water had given out; and all aboard were perishing with thirst. And it was agreed among master and crew that lots should be cast as to which of their number should be killed, that the others might slake their thirst with his blood. The lot fell upon the master—the Alasdair, after whom I was called.

That, at any rate, is the story as persistently told me by the old people of Sandwick, the village in the Outer Hebrides whence Alasdair hailed, and where reside many of my dearest kinsfolk at the present time. The tidings were brought home to Lewis by a Sandwick lad, a member of the crew, who survived to tell it. Although this happened nearly eighty years ago, the older natives of Sandwick still recount it at the ceilidhs with strange conviction.

To return to Applecross, it possessed no pier in the days of my childhood. Nor does it yet, for that matter. Then, as now, the mail-steamer, plying between Kyle of Lochalsh and the Outer Hebrides, sailed into Applecross Bay, and cruised offshore at a distance determined by weather conditions and the state of the tide. In the late afternoon she called on her voyage to Stornoway, discharging such passengers and cargo as were destined for Applecross and the adjacent townships by the shore, and embarking such as were travelling across the Minch to Lewis. In the early morning she again sailed into our bay, on her return trip. Twice every twenty-four hours, therefore, and in *most* weathers, she was met by a heavy ferryboat rowed out to her by Murdo MacRae and Murdo

Gillanders, the former the local joiner, the latter the tailor—two men who occupied a very important place in my early life.

To this day the two Murdos meet the Outer Isles steamer, as they did during my infancy at Applecross, nigh forty years ago, when one or other of them used to wrap me up in an oilskin, carry me aboard the ferryboat in his sinewy arms, and put me down on the stern thoft. The number of trips I actually made with them in this ferryboat, as they rowed out into the bay to meet the Hebridean mail-steamer, would be difficult to credit. Nothing ever deterred me from accompanying them. When wild seas beat upon our shore, or when the equinoctial gales visited us, the Murdos shrouded me in an old tarpaulin so stiff with the brine of storms that my fragile hands could scarcely bend it. This tarpaulin had the advantage of keeping me perfectly rigid when the ferryboat heaved and rolled in tempestuous water. On stormy days the waves broke over us, and smothered me. How I revelled in those wild days, those wild seas!

Murdo MacRae, a joiner to calling, as I have told you, was commissioned by my father to make me a model boat. This he did, and rigged her with sails. On less boisterous days it was my custom to trail this tiny craft at the stern of the ferryboat. My pride on the first occasion I towed her out to meet the steamer was tremendous. Even yet I can see Captain Cameron leaning over the bridge to congratulate me on my effort, and waving me a long adieu as the steamer sailed out to Lewis, and I towed my craft back to the shore.

On gusty days the Murdos always advised me to leave my model ship ashore. As Murdo MacRae lived next door to us, it was convenient for me to keep it in his shed. But one day, as we were returning to the shore, a squall brought a wave that swept our ferryboat from stem to stern, and carried away my boatie forever.

What immense pleasure that plaything gave me! How contented we used to be with the simple, and sometimes even crude, possessions of our tender years! A friend of mine in London often recalls the blissful days of childhood, when he hauled a wooden horse along the pavements of his native Paisley. His aunt had a haberdashery shop in that town; and one day she sprung a pleasant surprise on her little nephew by presenting him with a wee nose-bag she had knitted specially for the wee, wooden horse.

When visibility is good, it is possible to locate the mail-steamer thirty or forty minutes before she is due in the bay. When she comes in sight, it is easy for experienced seamen, having regard to the state of wind and tide, to estimate fairly accurately how soon the two Murdos should be stepping aboard the ferryboat, and rowing out to meet her.

One New Year's morning some years ago, the *Sheila*, after a quarter of a century's service between Kyle and Lewis, went ashore at Cuaig, near by, while on her return passage from Stornoway. A Dundee shipbreaking company bought the wreck, and salvaged anything of value, leaving her hulk, now lying barnacled and rusting at Cuaig. To this day someone sits on a knoll behind our old house at Milton, watching for the *Lochness*, the steamer now sailing the waters traversed so often by the *Sheila* of my childhood.

On this knoll at Milton I used to sit awhile with the ferrymen every afternoon, as they kept an outlook for the steamer. There I sang to them the first song with English words I ever knew, and a Jacobite song at that!

> "*Speed, bonnie boat, like a bird on the wing,*
> *Onward!" the sailors cry:*
> "*Carry the lad that's born to be king,*
> *Over the sea to Skye.*"

How fitting was this particular song to my early environment! Association of ideas had suggested it to my musical mother, since Skye lay but a few miles over the sea from our home at the Milton of Applecross, and every whiff of wind that came our way brought with it something of Prince Charlie. He might have passed along our shore-road but yesterday—so vivid were the reminiscences of his days of splendour, so tragic the memory of his defeat and exile.

* * * * *

Not only in song was I instructed, but also in poetry, and at an age when I understood less than half the words I could quote. Song was Mabel's province: poetry was the Colonel's. As he trailed me along the hill-path leading northward toward Loch Torridon, or southward by the fishing-villages of Camusteel and Camusterach toward the Crowlin Isles, he insisted on teaching me my first poem—Mrs. Hemans's *Graves of a Household.* It appealed to him because it reminded him so forcibly of his own people. He was now the only male member of his immediate family who had not met a violent and premature death. The graves of many of our kindred

> " . . . are scattered far and wide,
> By mount and stream and sea."

Long before I could go through the letters of the alphabet with any degree of accuracy, I could repeat every syllable of this poem.

From my veriest babyhood the Colonel sought to train my memory. At the age of three I could enumerate all the Books of the Old and New Testaments in their proper sequence, provided I was not interrupted while so doing. I recall being seated beside him on the scented hillside above the bay, while he drilled me into the rhythm of "Ecclesiastes, Song of Solomon, Isaiah, Jeremiah, Lamentations, Ezekiel", and assured me that by the following morning my diligence would enable me to tackle the third column, beginning with Daniel and concluding with Malachi. Somehow or other I did succeed in mastering the second column, though sunshine and sea sorely distracted me. My mind that day was more on Raasay Isle and Rona of the Seals than on learning to repeat, in parrot-like fashion, strings of names so meaningless to me that, not for a decade later, was I able to distinguish where one name ended and the following name began. I tried hard to divert my father's attention from such zeal for his infant son's learning, but with no avail. Concentration and tenacity of purpose were two of his chief characteristics. My rapture at the spouting whales, spotted from that sunlit hillside, could not deflect him. Greatly as he loved ships and everything pertaining to them, not even my sighting vessels sailing through the Sound would induce him to change the subject, until I was able to name, in their correct order, all the Books from Genesis to Ezekiel.

I also was obliged to commit to memory every word of the Shorter Catechism. But 'effectual calling' and the like conveyed nothing to me. They merely confused me. To be summoned, peremptorily, by word of mouth, was the most I ever could make of 'effectual calling'. Similar difficulties were presented by the Lord's Prayer and, at a later date, by many of those psalms, paraphrases, and hymns I was taught at Sunday-school. I understood about as much of what all this meant as did the child in the East End of London who, when asked by the teacher to repeat the Seventh Commandment, replied "Thou shalt not kick a duckery", and who, in reciting the Lord's Prayer, was heard to petition "And lead us not into Thames Station".

* * * * *

The Colonel discountenanced with stern demeanour any coddling or pampering of his offspring. He was resolved that we all should be hardy in spirit as well as in body. The natives of Applecross remember the occasion on which I, still a very wee boy, tripped on a stone when running about the old mill, and my father suddenly appeared on the scene just as I was on the point of bursting into tears.

"Don't cry, but *swear* as much as you like!" he roared, shaking his clenched fist at me with an air of grim authority. " Never let it be said that a MacGregor was seen crying ! "

Mention of swearing carries me in thought to the home-farm of Applecross, situated near a mill-dam, and tenanted at that time by the parents of our nurse, Bella MacKay. When I grew older, I sometimes was allowed to accompany Bella on her frequent visits to her people. In front of the MacKays' house ran a country road, on the opposite side of which grew two or three tall beeches, the roots of which protruded considerably from the soil, and disappeared in the bed of a tiny stream. It was the delight of my life to collect a canisterful of water from the stream, and pour it down through the great, exposed roots, in make-believe that I had constructed as good a mill-dam as that which drove the wheel some distance away. How shocked was the late Lady Middleton, as she was passing in her carriage one afternoon, by my insistence that she should alight to inspect my damn-mill !

* * * * *

One can readily imagine that life with a man as vigorous, as versatile, and as temperamental as the Colonel was never dull. It had its moments of depression as well as of mirth, its bouts and squalls as well as its interludes of calm and sunshine. But dulness, never ! And it certainly had its humorous side.

Once, while the Colonel was swimming at half tide in front of the house, he became so entangled in floating seaweed that he had to make for the jetty some distance away, when he wanted to come ashore. His clothes, however, lay among the rocks below the house. Noticing the nursemaid pushing the perambulator containing our very wee brother, Iain, he shouted to her in the Gaelic, directing her to carry his clothes to the jetty, toward which he was now swimming. But the nursemaid, a shy Highland lassie, was too covered with embarrassment to do anything of the kind. The more she dallied with the perambulator in his sight and within hearing of his shouting, the more incensed did he become. When enraged, he had a voice as powerful as Saint Columba's; and you remember what Adamnan said of Columba's voice!

The pandemonium reaching the shore from this solitary human being, modestly hiding the lower part of his person in the sea, and no one coming to succour him in his dilemma, was truly deafening. It soon brought the villagers out to see what was the matter. Eventually, Mabel came on the scene, and not a minute too soon. After explaining an aspect of the situation which he, in his impatience, had overlooked, she induced him to apologise to the wretched nursemaid. This he did with a laugh so hearty that everyone within sight, now aware of what had occurred, joined in laughter too.

Another humorous episode concerned a cask of stout which the Colonel had ordered from the south. As in the case of most merchandise, it had to come by the mail-boat. But a spell of boisterous weather prevented delivery. Day after day—nay, week after week—the *Sheila*, unable to disembark either passengers or cargo, sailed past to Stornoway, taking with her the stout for which, by this time, my father deliberately had worked up an unquenchable thirst. Likewise, in the small hours of each lawful day, she returned to Kyle, still carrying that cask. Each morning the Colonel tapped the barometer in the hope that it might indicate a change for the better: each afternoon found him at the study window, looking out over the stormy billows, and damning heavily, as the *Sheila's* lights disclosed her presence on the fringe of the bay, and she throbbing her way northward to Lewis, heedless of his exasperation.

At length the winds and seas abated somewhat. The Colonel now agreed with the ferrymen that, if they could manage to bring the cask ashore, he would celebrate the achievement in traditional fashion. Standing on the jetty, when at last they did return with it, was my father, anxious to take delivery and to implement his promise. He lent a hand with the unloading of the cask; and, while rolling it up the bumpy jetty to the roadside at Milton, he decided to celebrate there and then.

By this time the entire community was watching from its doors and windows, since the exploits of this unknown liquor, and its apparent determination to evade Applecross, had become one of the more important topics in the parish. Some of the more drouthy villagers were even on the spot.

And what was the upshot of all this? you may ask. Well, there was an upshot in more senses than one! Placing the cask on end, my father proceeded to remove the bung with the help of a stone picked up on the shore. With a mighty pop, up it went, and with it so great a column of frothy stout that all the astonished inhabitants could do was to stand by with open mouths, and watch the precious liquor soak the roadway at their feet. There they stood, helpless and gasping, thwarted as was Tantalus in classical times. My father could not but see the humour of the situation. After the exchange of a few observations, everyone laughed merrily, and proceeded to share out such dregs as the spouting fountain had left at the bottom of the cask.

CHAPTER II

DON

My First Dog

I WAS still but a child when, as I have said, my father commenced to train both my mind and my body in the direction in which he wished them to go. Frequently he trailed me so far afield that he was obliged to carry me all the way home in his arms. This meant nothing to him, since he was then a man in full vigour, to whom fatigue was unknown. Until within a year or two of his death at the age of eighty-four, he thought nothing of a twenty-mile walk twice or thrice weekly. Long walks were one of his methods of bringing up, or breaking in, his family to withstand the rigours of civilization, and the seasonal inclemencies of any land in which we might find ourselves. He seemed to live for the day when, unaided, I could accompany him on some of his more strenuous expeditions. To one who had cut his way through tropical forests, had tramped across deserts, and had climbed some of the world's highest peaks, the country around Applecross constituted no physical problem whatsoever, though a journey on foot into the trackless wilds of Torridon and Gairloch, lying away to the north of us, certainly called forth a degree of fortitude and endurance.

I recall clearly how I used to be trailed just a couple of hundred yards farther each day. With childish frenzy I allowed him to drag me past the point at which my exhaustion had necessitated our turning back the previous day. This hard training, this rigorous discipline, has stood me in good stead throughout life. It certainly contributed to my successes at the army sports in France during the last war.

In course of time I was able to walk as far as the house of one, Donald Bain, an elderly bachelor of considerable proportions, and factor for some landed property in the neighbourhood. Donald's house, the most generous building of its kind in the parish, stood on a flat promontory jutting out into the tideway. Near at hand was a sloping stone quay, for the most part covered with sea-wrack, and constructed for the purpose of enabling a puffer to discharge coal and stores for the landlord and his factor from time to time.

At Donald Bain's I usually was given sufficient time to recuperate from my trudge to help me to face at least the first few hundred yards of the homeward journey, since the Colonel and Donald always had ample to talk about. Furthermore, not infrequently did the former spend an hour or two in swimming out from the quay. But he and Donald whiled away more hours in converse than my father spent in the waters of the Sound. While they talked, I amused myself with Donald's dog, a female fox-terrier, smooth-haired. This creature would stand anything from me.

* * * * *

The Borrowing Days had come upon the Highlands, bringing with them their customary winds and rains. The sea lashed at our garden gate; and once more spume and spindrift were carried to our window-sills. The ferocity of this season of the year—known in the Highlands and Hebrides as the *Faoilteach*, or Storm-days—had prevented me from visiting Donald's for some weeks. With an improvement in the weather, however, I again took the shore-road with my father. On our arrival at Donald's, his housekeeper led me off to an out-house, where I found my little friend with a litter of the loveliest puppies. Never had I seen anything more marvellous, except perhaps the striped kittens our cat had in a box among rhubarb leaves at the foot of the garden. In a moment I was well into the centre of this nest of wee things, and they whimpering and scrambling all over me, the mother licking my face in maternal pride. When my father thought we should be making tracks for home, nothing would induce me to leave those puppies. I am told that I screamed and kicked, after the manner of recalcitrant children. Only on one condition would I go peacefully, namely, that one of them should be mine. My father and Donald stepped aside for a moment's conversation in the Gaelic. Donald then approached me in a grandfatherly way and, patting me on the cheek, told me that I could have my choice if I agreed to leave it until it was old enough to be taken from its mother. I agreed without a moment's hesitation, and in happy mood allowed my father to drag me home along the shore-road.

For the next week or two life in our home was unbearable. Without intermission I pestered my parents as to the earliest moment at which I could collect my treasure. The day began and ended with this enquiry.

"Jack, for heaven's sake take the child along to Donald's and let him bring the puppy home!" said my exasperated mother.

My insistence, I am sure, put me in possession of the creature some days before it normally would have been wrenched from its mother. I carried it home in my arms; and the Colonel carried us both.

The little dog grew up to be the most lovable companion. We put the name of Don on him, in remembrance of old Donald Bain. When the family removed to the other seaboard of Ross, Don naturally accompanied us. He and the Colonel (who had had the most devoted doggie friends in India and elsewhere) became inseparable. Once a week it was my father's custom to walk to the tip of a peninsula jutting out into the Dornoch Firth, just opposite the Doune of Creich, and roughly five miles from our new home at High Wind. As the shore was difficult to traverse in places, owing to muddy stretches and to sea-pools relieved only by springy hummocks of sea-pinks, he was in the habit of following the railway-line for more than half the journey. This line carried perhaps four trains daily in each direction—southward to Inverness, northward to Wick and Thurso. Halfway between home and the peninsula, Don and my father were on opposite sides of the line. An approaching train was heard. In his anxiety he called the dog to heel at the worst possible moment. His mangled body lay athwart the line when the train had passed. There was, indeed, a sorrowing home when, an hour or so later, he turned up with Don's broken body, to bury him in the garden where, but a few hours previously, he had been frolicking with the family. Death, we were assured, had been instantaneous.

This was the only occasion on which we ever saw our father shed a tear. That day's tragedy hung heavily upon him for many months. He felt he had placed upon the creature's loyalty and sense of obedience an obligation that meant certain death.

CHAPTER III

OUR NEIGHBOURS

I CANNOT say that I recall very clearly many of the villagers; and I have but the faintest recollections of the fisher-folk who, in rowing or sailing out from Camusteel and Camusterach, took me with them. But I do remember the deep sea-pools under the cliffs, where they dropped their lines and often drifted many hours before securing an adequate catch.

Of the inhabitants living in close proximity to us, however, such as the ferrymen and their families—and, of course, the miller—I have retained quite vivid remembrances. In a countryside so remote and sparsely populated, one shared with one's immediate neighbours a communal life so intimate as to give the impression that the other people of the world did not matter very much, if indeed they existed. At Milton we shared all the little worries and anxieties of our next-door neighbours, just as they shared ours. When the Colonel was in one of his furies, they made allowances, as we ourselves did when any of them failed to turn up at an appointed hour, or to execute a job of work as arranged. We all shared the same joys, and often the same sorrows. Our meals we regarded as common property. When the good things of life came our way, such as a barrel of apples, we divided them out, just as they, in turn, gave us of their catches of fish, or of the game poached by the more daring among the woods and hills.

A crowd of human beings one saw but once a week; and that was on Sundays, when the Auld Kirkers, the Free Kirkers, the United Frees, and the Free Presbyterians travelled on foot to their respective places of worship from neighbouring townships, or from their crofts among the fastnesses of the mountains. They always looked exceedingly glum, those first worshippers I ever saw apart from members of our own household. Their sharp, doctrinal differences, I imagine, may have exaggerated the gloom of their countenances when they came in contact with one another on the Sabbath. In reflecting upon them, I am reminded of the story so often recounted by way of illustrating the severity with which the Scots are said to regard the Lord's Day. One glorious summer's day a grave elder and a less grave youth set out together from their village on a ten-mile tramp to church. On and on they walked, without giving utterance to a syllable. But this doleful taciturnity was beginning to get on the youth's nerves; and he felt that, Sunday or no Sunday, one or other of them would have to break silence.

"It's a fine day," he ventured, unable to restrain himself any longer.

"Indeed, it *is* a fine day," replied the elder, with a gravity and solemnity calculated to smite the poor youth with the muteness of stone, "*but is this the day to be talking about days?*"

Nevertheless, our elders, in passing to and from the kirk, were not averse to casting a materialistic eye over their crops and beasts. They always looked a little ashamed, however, if detected in such worldiness.

I remember the green space on the hillside, not far from the sea, where the Free Presbyterians celebrated their communions in the open air in summer-time, and indeed may still do so, for all I know to the contrary. In the centre of this space was placed the communion table, on the boulders around which members of the congregation seated themselves. This simplicity in worship has surely much to commend it.

Incidentally, the seaboard of Wester Ross and of Sutherland, together with such of the Hebrides as lie approximately in the same latitudes, are the stronghold of the non-conforming Protestant Churches in the Highlands.

They certainly constitute the stronghold of the Free Church of Scotland. More applicable to Lewis and Harris and the north-west coast of the Scottish mainland than to any other part is the provocative rhyme said to have been used by Free Kirk supporters:

The Wee Kirk, the Free Kirk,
The Kirk wi'oot the Steeple:
The Auld Kirk, the Cauld Kirk,
The Kirk wi'oot the People.

In this region the very bell of the Free Church is believed to ring of a truer religion; while the organ is still regarded as a 'kist o' whustles'.

There was no intemperance at Applecross. Ours was a sober community. The natives occasionally had a thirst; but this was due mainly to their fare of salt herrings and tatties. I, too, had a thirst in those days. Sometimes I drank so much cold water that the Colonel feared diabetic tendencies. But the truth leaked out in the end: it was discovered that I had formed the habit of paying clandestine visits to the MacRaes whenever I learnt they were having salt herrings for dinner!

The hospitality of our secluded township was of the traditional order. This hospitality still persists throughout the greater part of the Highlands and Islands. To a large extent it explains how a modern French writer observed that the most fortunate thing about Scotland is the manner in which one can always arrive there in time for a meal.

The only occasion on which there was anything in the nature of a spree was when I handled my first box of matches. A huge bonfire had been piled up on the hillock between Milton and Camusteel; and one very dark night I was led out there, that I might have the distinction of setting it alight. Having had a box of matches placed in my tiny hands, I was allowed under strict supervision to strike one, and to hold it to some dry brushwood on the windward side. That was the first big conflagration I ever beheld. The occasion, I think, had something to do with Queen Victoria. Or was it connected with the Boer

War, that enterprise of which the Colonel disapproved so strongly?

One of the very first persons in the world, of whom I have any recollection, was Johann Finlayson, one of our maids. Johann was entrusted with the care of me when I set out to light the bonfire. She lived with an aged woman—possibly her mother—in a thatched cottage by the edge of our mill-loch. The thatch was very old. Upon it in great profusion grew ' Stinkie Willies ' and tufts of dog-grass. When Johann went home for an hour or so each afternoon, to do a turn for the old woman, she sometimes took me with her. Lying on a dresser, among a lot of higgledy-piggledy crockery, was a blue bag from which the auld buddy, on these occasions, used to give me a pickle of large sugar crystals. Indeed, a treat!

* * * * *

Next door, in the cottage immediately to the east of us, lived Mary Ann MacLure and her father. And what of my visits to their house do I recall more vividly than the hole in the floor of the wee, skylit attic above the kitchen? In this tiny apartment Mary Ann (as she herself reminded me when I revisited these haunts of childhood in 1939) sat long hours with her needle. By the fireside stood the poker which I used to enjoy thrusting through the hole in the floor. Often it dropped into the kitchen below, sometimes among the dishes, but never, fortunately, on the head of either of the MacLures. Occasionally, when Mary Ann would be at her sewing and I at my capers, some irresistible power pulled the poker through the hole. How this happened, I never could understand. Instantly I rushed downstairs to the kitchen, in the hope of solving the mystery. Since there was no trace of the poker anywhere, I began to suspect that this might have been yet another manifestation of the Black Devil dwelling in the mill so close at hand.

It was Mary Ann herself who told me recently how her old father, on noticing the point of the poker protruding from the kitchen ceiling, used to seize hold of it and mysteriously pull it through from my fingers.

Almost as fascinating as the hole in the floor was the sandglass on the kitchen mantelshelf, by which Mary Ann timed the boiling of eggs. Though clocks and watches were by no means scarce in our home, and I had seen many similar timepieces in the homes of others, that thread of sand, rushing so delicately, so imperceptibly, was the medium through which I first became conscious of the passage of time. An egg timed by any other method never tasted quite the same to me.

* * * * *

Then there was Sandy, whose surname I do not think I ever knew.

Between thirty and forty years ago sanitary arrangements were even less common in rural Scotland than they are to-day. It happened that Mabel had given instructions for the installation in an outhouse of a modern convenience that had to come all the way from Shanks's celebrated pottery at Barrhead. Plumbers at Applecross were as inexperienced as they were scarce. That this weighty commodity—this veritable monument in porcelain—might be brought into use, we were obliged to call upon Sandy's services. One day, when the unveiling ceremony seemed imminent, Sandy was standing on the seat, fiddling with the ball-cock in the cistern near the ceiling of the outhouse. Meanwhile I persisted in annoying him by poking him at intervals with a shepherd's crook, and then running away before he could catch me. When I returned to have another good jab at him, his foot slipped. Down it plunged into the inmost recesses of the porcelain. Since he was a fellow of quite considerable proportions, he went with no uncertainty.

My hilarious laughter at the plight of poor Sandy brought our maids to the backyard to find him well and truly trapped. He was endeavouring to undo his bootlace, hoping to release his foot. But in vain. So the local blacksmith had to be summoned. He arrived with a sledge-hammer, and with one mighty blow set Sandy free, shattering Mabel's hygienic dreams.

* * * * *

Unable in those days to distinguish between *meum* and *teum*, I developed a propensity for petty thieving. At the end of the village was the local emporium, kept by Mrs MacRae, then a woman in her sixties. She loved me dearly when I was a child; and she had no feelings whatsoever about my slipping behind the counter to help myself to anything that took my fancy. She also ran the inn; and she was a devoted church-worker, forby. But the liberty she extended to me behind the counter soon grew upon me. My taste varied between sweeties and dried fruits. The latter were marketed then in a form less delectable than that in which they are purveyed nowadays. Nevertheless, the box of prunes, standing alternately in the window among the flies of summer, or on the floor amid paper shavings, disused cardboard containers, and the sweepings of a decade or two, sorely tempted my eye—so sorely, indeed, that my internal capacity could never quite keep pace with it. Each time I raided that box, I carried away twice as many prunes as I could consume. I wore a little kilt of MacGregor tartan, and a flaming red jersey. Such prunes as I had loosened, but could not accommodate immediately, either in my mouth or in both hands, were systematically wound round in the folds of the jersey. Of these depredations I knew Mrs MacRae was aware. She *must* have noticed when my cheeks and jersey bulged. I am certain, also, that at times she even watched my small fingers tearing away at the prunes that I sometimes found to have been packed more tightly than rendered entirely pleasurable my frequent sorties behind the counter. Had she checked me, instead of aiding and abetting, she might have done something to prevent the pilfering incidents of which, in subsequent years, I was oftener found guilty than not proven!

Mrs MacRae's husband, Sandy, was as sandy-coloured as a boy, when he died in 1927, at the age of ninety-one.

He and his *cailleach* were inseparable. They had no children of their own, which may explain the latitude they allowed me. Together, for half a century, they were occupied with church work. They threw in their lot with what was then the United Free Church of Scotland. From its inception they laboured faithfully for its welfare. The photographs of ministers and missionaries, whom they knew personally, filled the inn parlour almost to overflowing. Their knowledge of ecclesiastical matters was amazing. And so diligently did they read such publications as *The Record* that they could tell you all that was to be known about the mission-fields of Livingstonia and Calabar.

Mrs MacRae, for all her virtues, had one serious fault—that of charging to her customers' accounts articles they had not purchased. Repeated detection failed to make any impression on her method of book-keeping. Some years before her death, however, there came to the parish a newly appointed doctor, whose wife soon set herself to terminate this imposition, so far as she and her household were concerned. Times without number she remonstrated with Mrs MacRae at the persistent occurrence on her bill of articles she never had had. But her protestations were useless. So doctor and wife resorted to keeping a private account. When Mrs MacRae submitted her account hereafter, they simply deleted from it articles not appearing on their own list, and paid accordingly. This arrangement worked admirably for some time. But one day there occurred an item that incensed them—" Pail, 6/9." They had stood a good deal. But six-and-ninepence for an imaginary pail they would not tolerate.

Buoyed up with righteous indignation, they now made for ' The Street ', resolved to put an end to this imposition. On entering the shop, they assured Mrs MacRae that at no time during their stay at Applecross had they made such a purchase. When they had exhausted both themselves and their store of vituperation, Mrs MacRae, who meanwhile had remained in silence behind the counter, confident under her mutch that she could deal with the situation, folded her arms and assumed an air of quiet composure. Then, keeking over her specs, she delivered herself in those plaintive tones so characteristic of the people of Wester Ross: "Well, well! Believe me or believe me not, *someone* got a pail!"

Faced with a retort as convincing as this, both the doctor and his wife were inarticulate.

On the road to Applecross—Loch Kishorn on a hazy day, with the Pass of the Kine in the background

" The Dornie Ferry . . . delighted me in those days "

CHAPTER IV

WHALES AND SEALS

IT WAS at Applecross, though perhaps in a somewhat elementary way, that I first became familiar with the birds and beasts of our fields, of our woodlands, and of the vast moorlands and mountains comprising our formidable background: here, furthermore, I was introduced to those strange creatures inhabiting the sea—our foreground, as it were.

I could not have been more than two or three years old when I became painfully conscious that animals were capable of feeling, and were remarkably sensitive to pain and distress.

Sometimes my parents drove by pony and trap to Lochcarron to visit friends in that neighbourhood, or to Stromeferry, four miles farther south. Stromeferry was the original terminus of the railway running westward across Ross-shire from Dingwall, until the line was extended a year or two later as far west as Kyle of Lochalsh. Passengers from the north—from the Applecross and Torridon regions—came by road, and entrained at the tiny wayside station known as Strathcarron. In any case, whether my parents were bound for Strathcarron or for Stromeferry, it was a terrific undertaking for a pony. As I usually accompanied them on these excursions over the mountains, I became increasingly sensitive to the strain that our travel must have placed on an animal committed to drag up the Pass of the Kine, and through these untamed wilds, a trap containing two fairly heavy adults and one infant, and often some luggage to boot. Out of sympathy for the pony I used to scream at the foot of one of the worst pulls, in order to be allowed to alight, and give the pony what very little assistance I could in trailing his ponderous load to the summit. "Lift the child down, Jack!" Mabel used to say in irritation. "He soon will wish he had remained where he was."

It is true that, far from my having been a help, I was a hindrance, since I could not push the trap uphill for more than a couple of feet ere I became so exhausted that I just had to hang on to the back step, and be dragged up until the pony was halted for a few minutes' rest. My antics, I fear, sometimes necessitated our stopping the pony on a steep acclivity, thus placing on the poor beast an additional expenditure of energy in starting off again.

Yet, I could not but revel in those excursions among so much of the grandest scenery in Britain—Loch Kishorn and Loch Carron, Loch Alsh and Loch Long and lovely Loch Duich; Glen Shiel and the Five Sisters of Kintail; the tidal narrows at Strome, or between Kyle and Kyleakin; the towering crags of Skye; the road over the Mam Ratagan traversed by Dr Johnson and James Boswell on their adventurous journey to Glenelg. Though this road is reputed to be one of the finest hill routes in the British Isles, I have always considered it tame in comparison with the *bealach* linking Applecross with the world.

The ferry at Dornie, recently superseded, alas! by a bridge spanning the tides at the entrance to Loch Long, delighted me in those days. With great caution our pony footed the cobblestones of the jetty when we crossed here on our way to visit the Colonel's friends in Kintail. And, in listening to his stories of Kintail and of the wild MacRaes (he would never allow that the MacRaes were a clan in the true sense!), I gazed in amazement at the weathered shell of Eilean Donan Castle, near by. I remember his reciting the doings of the wily MacKenzies of Kintail, to whom Eilean Donan belonged in olden times, and of the MacRaes, its Constables. I also remember his trying to enlist my interest in the old controversy regarding the position of the MacRaes in clan history. Had the chiefship, *if any*, descended strictly in accordance with ancient

Celtic Law? That was one of the burning topics in the Highlands in those days; and even yet the most fanatical arguments are engendered by it. I was very young to be burdened with such matters; but the Colonel believed it was as important that I should know something of them as that I should be familiar with the Scriptures. Clan controversy I found less diverting, however, than his account of how Eilean Donan became the headquarters of the Jacobite forces assembled in 1719 for the almost forgotten rising inspired the previous year by Philip of Spain. Spanish troops numbering between forty and fifty garrisoned the Castle then; and they were all taken prisoner when the *Worcester*, one of the Hanoverian ships of war, bombarded it, and reduced it to the ruins I knew in childhood. With all this local history I was *au fait* before I could read my first primer.

Roughly a quarter of a century later—in the summer of 1932—I dashed up from London to Kintail, at the invitation of the late Colonel MacRae-Gilstrap and as special correspondent to *The Times*, to the opening ceremony, after the Castle's restoration. Colonel MacRae-Gilstrap, who had purchased the ruins twenty years before, claimed to be hereditary Constable in succession to his grandfather seven times removed, the Rev. Farquhar MacRae, who, between the years 1618 and 1651, was both minister of Kintail and Constable of the Castle. My father, however, questioned whether the office of Constable at Eilean Donan was ever *hereditary*, with the result that MacRae-Gilstrap and he were at loggerheads for years.

* * * * *

My juvenile concern for the welfare of animals awoke in me a corresponding curiosity about their ways, about their modes of living—some rudimentary interest in natural history.

Associated with Applecross in my tender years were whales, those strange and monstrous people—those denizens of the deep—who wander about our oceans, and sometimes even lose their way among our islands. Shall I ever forget the impression created on me the first time I saw one of these tremendous mammals break the surface of our sea with his nose, and watched him blow? Shall I ever forget the day when the backwash of a huge whale left me high and dry? The Colonel was swimming gaily at some distance from the shore, while I remained seated where he had deposited me—in shallow water about a couple of yards from the tide's edge. On realising what had caused the wave that sent me aground among slippery stones, I yelled to my father in great excitement, fearful lest the whale might gobble him up. That very morning, as it happened, when reading aloud from The Book at family-worship, he had come again to the passage about Jonah that always interested me so much; and I now felt apprehensive lest a similar fate awaited *him*!

Whales frequently disported themselves in our bay, investigating it when travelling through the Sound dividing us from Raasay and Skye. From the top of a precipitous cliff overlooking our western sea, whither my father had trailed me on one of his training exploits, I once observed a school of no fewer than five of these monsters, ploughing beneath the water as swiftly as any ship in those days could steam on the surface. This was the most stupendous piece of movement I had witnessed hitherto. The mail-boat, in all conscience, was a huge thing in my sight at that time—a huge thing to have the power of motion, I thought. Five monster whales, however, moving rapidly in echelon formation, so close inshore, bewildered me by their bulk and power, and by the ridiculous ease with which they appeared to propel themselves. I was amazed when, in rhythmic succession, they tore the surface of the sea with their gleaming dorsal fins, or spouted heavenward from their blow-holes tall columns of condensed moisture, as whales do with a roaring sound when exhaling breath. Each time part of a whale's back came in view, it gave one the impression of its being but the merest fragment of the arc of some gigantic wheel, turning and turning perpetually underwater with a terrific stride. My infant mind could not comprehend such wonders of the deep. The Colonel often reminded me in later years that I cried inconsolably at this pageantry of bulk, of power, and of movement, not because of any fear the whales had instilled in me, but because the spectacle had mystified me so.

* * * * *

Schools of porpoises came our way too; and I recall my attempts at counting them as they birled past. But I never enjoyed the visits of the whales and porpoises as much as of those soft-eyed, silken seals, emissaries from the Courts of the Kings of Lochlann, as we say in the Isles, and kinsfolk of the elusive Clan MacCodrum. They visited us rather spasmodically. The local fisher-people disliked their coming because they spoilt the fishing, and sometimes destroyed the nets, and also because, as a rule, their venturing close inshore signified the approach of bad weather.

But, oh! the joy those wondering-eyed darlings gave me! When they lingered by our shore, I felt myself in serene and friendly company. An old bull seal remained for weeks by the rocks below our garden, heedless of my endeavours to shoo him away. And I often reflect on the hours spent by our garden's sea-gate, singing to a young seal who, eventually, became so accustomed to me that he would bob and frolic in the shallowing tide at my very feet, and sometimes even paddle ashore to view me at close quarters. When I sang to him the few melodies I knew at that age, he answered me back in seal-music. And that was long before the late Marjory Kennedy-Fraser reduced *The Seal-woman's Croon* to staff notation for us! One song in particular my seal friend liked was *The Blue-bells of Scotland*. I do not think he understood the words, since at that age I, myself, scarcely followed them sufficiently to have been able to impart their meaning. With the melody, however, I was perfectly familiar; and I could repeat the words, whether I actually understood them or not:

O where, tell me, where is your Highland laddie gone?
O where, tell me, where is your Highland laddie gone?
He's gone wi' streaming banners, where noble deeds are done;
And it's, oh! in my heart I wish him safe at home.

O where, tell me, where does your Highland laddie dwell?
O where, tell me, where does your Highland laddie dwell?
He dwells in bonnie Scotland, where blooms the sweet bluebell;
And it's, oh! in my heart I lo'e my laddie well.

The creek below our garden became his favourite playground. I so envied him his faculty for movement—his power of expression—in a medium in which, as yet, I had had but little experience. His activities created in me a sense of pure, unadulterated delight.

Although I was nearly drowned on several occasions, I probably owe my confidence in water not so much to astrology(!!) as to my upbringing by the shores of the Western Highlands, and to my eagerness to compete with those seals that used to come up with shiny heads to look at me, snorting gently in so doing, and dilating their nostrils while taking a deep breath before submerging again. With their glittering eyes they seemed to be enticing me to come and join them in the sea, as though I had been one of their MacCodrum kindred. The other thing that contributed toward my familiarity with water as an element in which I can move swiftly was my determination that one day I should be able to follow my aquatic father out into the open sea where, for an hour or two daily, he derived so much joy in which I was then too young to participate.

All this and more I remember of Applecross—the tumultuous crying of seabirds in time of storm—the weird screaking and squawking of gulls perched on our chimney-pots at Milton—the ceaseless and inevitable coming and going of the tides—the smell of wet wrack at the ebb—the sea's edge, a strange longing for which has followed me all through life, and is requited only when I travel to the Outer Hebrides to sojourn with my kinsfolk there.

* * * * *

To revert to the seals and the Seal-folk, traditions concerning them are still to be found in these parts. They are most prevalent, of course, in North Uist, and in the isles scattered about the Sound of Harris. North Uist is the home of the MacCodrums of the Seals, a sept of the illustrious Clan Ranald of the Isles.

Though for the most part the Seal-folk is believed to have come from Lochlann (Norway), this particular clan is said to have sprung from a progenitor who, while wandering by the shore of his Hebridean isle, chanced to find a number of seals in process of shedding their coats. Off dashed MacCodrum with one of the skins. When on the point of hiding it above the lintel of his cottage, its owner followed him in. This seal-woman he now prevented from returning to the sea. He clothed her with raiment like that worn by ordinary human beings in the Isles, and eventually married her. She bore him a large *clann* or family, which became known throughout the Hebrides, and even in Ireland, as the Children of MacCodrum of the Seals. However, there came a day when MacCodrum was away from home, and his wife searched the house for her seal-skin. She found it tucked away above the lintel, and, donning it, rejoined her sea kindred. When MacCodrum returned, the empty hidie-hole told its own story.

The connection between the Seal-folk and the MacCodrums still persists in the minds of many of the older inhabitants of the Outer Hebrides, more especially, perhaps, among those dwelling in North Uist, or in the isles lying in that great tide-race, the Sound of Harris. On one of these isles—on Berneray, actually—a branch of the Seal-folk settled a century or two ago; and the fishermen of the Outer Isles assure us that the sleeky, soft-eyed descendants of this branch may be seen to this day in the Sound of Berneray, the channel separating the Isle of Berneray from North Uist.

Popular belief has it that the MacCodrums were seals by day and human beings by night. And, since the Mac-

Codrums were aware of their origin, they took great care never to injure a seal.

It was because the natives of western Ireland regarded the seals as metamorphosed humans that they were at such pains not to molest them. The MacCodrums of the Hebrides, on the other hand, were deferent to seals not merely on account of their human origin, but because they believed them to be of their own flesh and blood—their very own kith and kin.

And I must just say a word in passing about the *lachs*, or widgeons, that went skimming across our bay, and at times searched the dulse below the sea-gate at the foot of our garden. Their forbears, a sept known as the Clan MacAndy, also came from Berneray waters. Like their neighbours, the MacCodrums, they fell 'under spell'. Touched by a Druid wand, they were turned into *lachs*, the long-tailed ducks of the Sound of Harris.

CHAPTER V

MY FIRST SCHOOL

WE WERE living at High Wind (Ardgay), in Easter Ross, when I first went to school. And you may recollect that I mention in *The Goat-Wife* how I was suddenly and mercilessly precipitated into this new and strange environment. I had locked Jessie away in an old trunk while playing at circuses, and had forgotten all about her! She was almost asphyxiated when discovered. To having such an impossible child about the house any longer, school was the only alternative. The idea of my being sent off to the local parish school had always been a little repugnant to my mother; and it is just possible that my father, for all his democratic leanings, may also have had some feelings in the matter. But the trunk episode readily bereft them of any serious qualms in this connection. Forthwith I was packed off to the village school at Gledfield. With unusual haste arrangements were completed for my enrolment.

My recollections of this first school are numerous. Within a radius of fifty miles or so, the schoolmaster was nickednamed Boxer, or Gee Gee. His real name was George Gordon MacLeod. The title of Boxer he probably earned through the frequency with which he boxed the ears of the scholars committed to his charge. Speaking personally, I found him a vicious old devil, though I can well understand that to others he may have been quite charming. Even at that early age I regarded him as utterly unsuited for the care of children, and deplorably lacking in that humanity which ought to be a prerequisite of those entrusted with the education of the young. Boxer was not without his good points, however. He was a strict teetotaller; and he never smoked. Not in the most furious of his furies—not in the most tempestuous of his tempers—was he ever known to have used a swear-word. Other utterances, however, were more dumbfounding than a good damn or two would have been. Owing to his mastery of the Gaelic, he had a considerable advantage over anyone by whom he was enraged, since he frequently blasted with great effect in his mother-tongue, which his victims probably did not understand, and which actually could be more telling—more devastating—than a few mild expletives in English.

Gee Gee was a Gaelic scholar of some distinction, and with the Colonel shared the belief that Gaelic was the language of the Garden of Eden. The suggestion that this, perhaps, explained why Adam and Eve were ejected from the Garden has always annoyed Gaelic fanatics. Jokes about the Gaelic they regard as being impious as jokes about 'The Word'. Like the Colonel, he never spoke in English to anyone able to converse with him in the Gaelic. Whereas all his school-children were taught Gaelic songs, his own daughters were given an extra dose, with the result that the eldest always had to sing a Gaelic song or two at the Land League social gatherings in the village hall. It took her nearly forty minutes to get through one particularly popular song, the chorus of which had to be repeated after each of the thirty-eight verses—composed by one of the minor bards thrown up by the land agitation in the Highlands during the latter half of the nineteenth century.

Boxer in his heyday was a prominent Liberal and Land Leaguer. On more than one occasion he was invited to stand for Parliament in the Land Reform interest, which has always been an excellent electioneering topic in the Highlands, but has never really got anywhere, largely because its advocates have seldom possessed more than a superficial knowledge of the fundamental part played by land within the capitalist economy. But Gee Gee's parliamentary hopes never materialised. His large family was too great a handicap. In those days only persons with private means could compete for political honours.

Yet, how do you think this intrepid Land Leaguer completed his public career? On his retiral from schoolmastering, he became factor to Sir Charles Ross, at Balnagown—the landed proprietor claiming, among much else, the very parish in which his school was situated. After all he had uttered and written about landlords in general, and about poor Charles in particular, this appointment was a little difficult to understand. "Traitor! Traitor!" exclaimed his former cronies. "Snake in the grass!" declared my father, who had kept in touch with John MacPherson and John Murdoch and other prominent Radicals throughout his many years' absence from this country. But, as one of Boxer's daughters explained to me, "beggars can't be choosers!" His installation at Balnagown, where he was now entrusted with the task of making a success of a land system he had spent forty vehement years of his life in discrediting, was certainly a God-send to his large family, for whom he could not possibly have provided on his meagre retiral pension. The teacher of to-day has little conception of the drudgery and impecuniosity of the teacher of thirty years ago, especially in the more remote areas.

* * * * *

My first school-day was a Friday. So thrilled and enchanted was I by its novelty that, unduly early the following morning, when on my way to school again, I called for the stationmaster's children, and was a little puzzled to learn that they were not even out of bed. Picture my disappointment when their mother put her head out of the window to inform me that there was no school on Saturdays! Although all our maids had attended this village school at one time or another, this fact seemed to have escaped their memory.

School brought me into contact with such realities as addition and subtraction. The intricacies of multiplication and division loomed some days ahead. A sense of inferiority seized me on realising that I was the only member of the infant-room incapable of adding together a few simple digits. In point of fact, not only was I younger than the bright things in this department, but I had been dumped among them toward the end of a session.

I treated my first school-day as a sort of social function. A good deal of the time I talked, addressing all manner of embarrassing questions to the mistress. I saw no reason why I should not be as normally garrulous in school as elsewhere. My interjections caused considerable mirth and tittering among the other scholars. (*Pupils* were unheard of in the Highlands in those days: all children attending board schools were *scholars*.)

On my second day I was a little more restrained. I talked less. My energies were now concentrated more on elementary arithmetic than on babbling, since I hated my inability to do the simple things the others did with such ease.

When a new girl was enrolled a few days later, leapt on her seat, clapped her hands in great excitement, and punctuated the droving of a flock of sheep down the country road, just outside the schoolroom window, with " Dogs barking! Dogs barking! ", I joined in the general ridicule of her, and became aware, in so doing, that a similar demonstration on my own part had evoked much giggling a day or two previously. I had now become 'class-conscious'.

On my third day at Gledfield, Boxer overheard me call a boy a limmer in the stony playground. Never before this day had I heard this strange word. Willie Fraser, a much older boy, had used this epithet to me on our way to school that morning; and what was more natural than that I should add this choice word to my own somewhat limited vocabulary? Since the natives of this part of Ross pronounce the letter, i, in words like limmer, as though it were u, Boxer was positive that I had called my classmate by another word of two syllables—a name beginning with b, and referred to by Horace Smith in his *Tin Trumpet* as a term of endearment commonly used among sailors! Thereupon he dragged me forth by the ear, and cast me into the passage connecting the main schoolroom and the schoolhouse, and leading to the spooky coal-cellar and the cupboard where Bathie, the school-cleaner, kept her brushes and dusters. In that diabolical Kingdom of Goblin he inflicted on me some measure of sadistic pain, until my head rang and my senses reeled. Soon I was overcome by the most frightening claustrophobia. His inquisition went the length of trying to get me to admit that I had used the term of endearment alluded to. Unsuccessful in this, he left me there in utter darkness for what appeared to be a very long time. I was terror-stricken. That episode left a bad flavour. From that day I detested Boxer and everything pertaining to his wretched school. Henceforth I rejoiced with the more unruly scholars who, in wandering home from school, did not emulate Wordsworth's primrose-plucking children, but went shouting along the country road:

Boxer, Boxer, blow your horn :
All the scholars are in the corn !

I did not tell Boxer that Willie Fraser had committed an even greater misdemeanour: he actually had called me a bastard. What evil might have befallen me in that dark, foreboding passage, had I been overheard using *that* elegant expression, I leave to your imagination. In the Scottish Highlands 'bastard' was deemed the most frightful word human lips could utter. This is curious, bearing in mind that the Highlands have always been notorious for bastardy. The word, illegitimate, one never heard in those times, except among the more educated orders, who *whispered* it.

Whenever I hear that word so familiar to sailors and to Horace Smith, association of ideas carries me back to Willie Fraser in the playground, and to Boxer twisting my ear in that passage. It was a long time before I felt I could forgive Willie for his having introduced me to a term which, when innocently repeated, should have resulted in my being cast into Boxer's dark prison! In revenge, I crept into the garden of the cottage where he lived with his parents, and stole some red gooseberries, and pulled up by the roots a huge cluster of apple-ringie growing by the doorstep. Willie is now inspector of police at Stornoway, where I see him from time to time. But he is much too formal and correct now to use such rude words!

Gee Gee kept his own family of six or seven daughters as much under his thumb as he did his scholars. Isabel, the youngest of his brood, caught in the act of whispering in the class (one of the most heinous crimes known to mankind!), was ignominously ordered out of the room, and placed behind the door in that same grim passage. When I met Isabel in Kelso recently, after a lapse of thirty years, I happened to mention, during our exchange of reminiscences, the matter of my banishment over the word, limmer.

"Och!" said she, "that's nothing. He once put me out there early in the day, and forgot all about me. I might have been there yet, if Bathie had not found me when she came to get the broom to sweep the schoolroom floor."

Poor old Bathie! She is dead many years, resting from her life-long labours with brooms and dusters and mops. She lived all her days in one room, near the Free Church. That room was the darkest and dreariest I was ever in. So wrinkled was she that we believed her to be about two hundred years old. One might see her o' mornings, going to the well near by, carrying a pail in one hand and, in winter-time, an axe in the other, to break the ice on the well.

* * * * *

The school-day opened with prayer, conducted exclusively by Boxer himself. He was expert at the praying. For this ordeal all the children, including the veriest infants, were assembled in the main part of the building. After prayers, a certain proportion of which was done in the Gaelic, we had a quarter of an hour of Curwen's Tonic Sol-fa, an invention that, from the point of view of music, should have been suppressed at its inception.

So universal and persistent has been the teaching of this solfeggio that to this day the Highlanders remain largely ignorant of staff notation, and have a somewhat crude conception of what constitutes music. This is well illustrated by the vocal exhibitions of so many Gaelic singers appearing as medallists and winners of sundry prizes at Highland concerts all over the country, with pianoforte accompaniment consisting of nothing more than a primitive vamping. When these performers play their own or one another's accompaniments, the effect is frightful!

Up and down that long scale with the large and small print we travelled in a variety of screeches, times without number, and in and out of it at erratic intervals. Thereafter the taller children ranged themselves on the back forms of the main schoolroom, while the infants crawled about in front. The entire muster then rasped its discordant way through a Gaelic song or two.

Then we were given our quota of imperialistic ideology. This was administered for the most part through the singing of such patriotic productions as *Rule, Britannia* and *Britannia, the Pride of the Ocean*. And, since Kipling had never been heard of in our parish, the singing of patriotic songs was followed by an hour with *Casabianca*, or perhaps with Cowper's lines on the foundering of the *Royal George*, with Kempenfelt and others aboard. We were much touched by the heroism of the boy on the burning deck, though his unhappy plight presented a gruesome picture to our young minds.

Looking back, it would appear as though everything we were taught to sing or recite had to do with wars and victories and disasters of one kind or another on land and sea—always something of a naval or military character in which the enemy got the end he deserved. Air heroics were then unknown since Bleriot as yet had not flown the Channel.

But just think of a wee, Highland laddie having to remember a big, ugly word like Kempenfelt!

How subtle, I have thought since, was all this imperialist teaching, served up so popularly in song and verse to young people, the majority of whom were destined in after-life to be crofters, ploughmen, and carters. That it had the desired effect, however, is shown by the numbers who rushed off to the Great War. It was from humble parishes such as ours that divisions like the Fifteenth Scottish and Fifty-first Highland were recruited. To the tune of *Britannia, the Pride of the Ocean*, we sang quite different words when we got overseas, and strove as best we could to cheer ourselves on those interminable route-marches from one battle-front to another. All I now remember of those words are the following, from what might be described as the refrain:

At the halt, on the left, form platoon!
At the halt, on the left, form platoon!
If the odd numbers don't mark time two paces,
How the hell can the rest form platoon?

When eventually I went to school at Edinburgh, I found the same teaching there, with the difference that it now had to be paid for. But I never had much aptitude for memorising verse about the Battles of This and of That—the Nile, Baltic, Trafalgar, Corunna, Balaclava—and was reduced to despair by my efforts to assimilate compositions extolling bugles and battles, victories and national bravados, and naval engagements in which, with the help of Divine Intervention, we always blew the other fellow to bits. One might have forgiven the responsible authorities had they taught us G. K. Chesterton's *Lepanto*, for, although it is not necessarily great poetry, it certainly is fine ballad, full of colour and pageantry. But one could not pardon them for their insistence that class after class, decade after decade, should endure the mediocrity of *The Burial of Sir John Moore*. Little wonder we relieved the monotony of these verses with schoolboy jokes about those 'sods with their bayonets turning'!

Recitations were taught in exactly the same way as songs. In parrot-like fashion the entire class repeated the verse after the teacher, in unison, line by line. How we used to grind out:

I once had a sweet little doll, dears,
The prettiest doll in the world ;
Her cheeks were so red and so white, dears,
And her hair was so charmingly curled.
But I lost my poor little doll, dears,
As I played in the heath one day ;
And I cried for more than a week, dears,
But I never could find where she lay.

I found my poor little doll, dears,
As I played in the heath one day ;
Folks say she is terribly changed, dears,
For her paint is all washed away,
And her arms trodden off by the cows, dears,
And her hair not the least bit curled ;
Yet, for old sake's sake she is still, dears,
The prettiest doll in the world.

I was grown up before I knew the origin of these lines. One day I happened to be scanning Charles Kingsley's *Water Babies*; and there, to my surprise, were the lines that boys and girls alike had to memorise at Gee Gee's school. How odd, I now thought it, that the boys of a Highland parish, who neither possessed nor desired dolls, should have been obliged to learn verses so obviously written for little girls!

There were other lines, however, into which we all hurled ourselves with amazing verve and volume, and which, in comparision with rhapsodies on dolls and Kempenfelts, awoke in me something more in consonance with my temperament—those lines ascribed to one, William Allingham:

Up the airy mountain,
Down the rushy glen,
We daren't go a-hunting,
For fear of Little Men ;
Wee folk, good folk,
Trooping all together,
Green jacket, red cap,
And grey-cock's feather !

* * * * *

Many of the children attending Gee Gee's school were as wild as the moorland leveret. Whenever they took it into their heads, they played truant among the hills and woods, their whereabouts known not even to their parents. Not that the parents always minded. Fathers accustomed to a bit of poaching now and then were quite flattered when one or more of their unruly, untameable offspring took a day or two off to go poaching on their own, arriving home long after dark with rabbits and hares, salmon and game-birds. Their absence from school, and sometimes even from the parish, often lasted several days, until in the end the school attendance officer, or his equivalent, succeeded in rounding them up. The reputation gained by our parish of Kincardine for its juvenile poachers was truly remarkable, though there were gamekeepers galore. It always seemed strange to us that the staple diet of so many gamekeepers' families was rabbit, when they themselves might so easily have done a little poaching. A few years ago a Tain boy was sent for his summer holidays to the home of a gamekeeper at High Wind. Day after day he was served up with rabbit in one form or another, until it fairly scunnered him. He took ill at length; and medical aid had to be summoned. The doctor prescribed a dose of castor oil. The boy suggested that a *ferret* would have been more appropriate!

It is curious how the country-bred boy often revels in killing. Give him a gun, and you have given him all he wants in heaven. He regards shooting as the most manly occupation on earth. The story is told of some rural children attending Sunday-school in the east of Scotland. When asked by the minister what they would like to do when they went to heaven, one of them replied: " Please, sir, I wud like tae play the hairp."

" Please, sir," said another, " I wud like tae sing psalms."

" Please, sir, I wud like tae be aside Abraham," answered a third.

" And what would *you* like to do, Davie, when you go to heaven? " enquired the minister.

"Please, sir, I wud jist like tae stot aboot wi' God, and shoot rabbats!"

Members of a family of poaching sons we knew absented themselves in relays from the advantages of education so generously provided by the State. Thus they maintained a well-filled pot for the home. They had to travel no more than a few hundred heathery yards from their doorstep to reach the outskirts of the Gledfield pinewoods, which were so dense that young truants, accustomed to life in the open, might have evaded detection therein for weeks. When tired of harrying the woods, they had not far to go to the salmon-pools of the River Carron. To find every eligible member at school the same day was recognised in the parish as a physical impossibility; and many a laugh they occasioned when supplying the teacher with excuses for their absence. If a stranger approached their croft, guilty consciences sent half the clan into hiding in the interstices of the byre, until the opportunity arose for a sudden dash to concealment in the heather, or in the pine-woods beyond. For years attempts to assemble the entire brood failed. However, I believe that on one occasion the minister nearly succeeded in enumerating them all at one time. Noticing the barefooted soles of the youngest, as they protruded from beneath a zinc bath-tub lying upside down by the garden gate, he tickled them with the end of his walking-stick. They were quickly withdrawn from view; and he had not the heart to discover the wee, wild thing thereunder. He found himself in much the same position with regard to this family as did another minister, who made repeated attempts to baptize the children of a shepherd dwelling remotely among the mountains of Skye. On the approach of a stranger, these youngsters fled. Time after time the minister journeyed to their homestead, in the hope of baptizing some at least: time after time he returned without getting within arm's length of one of them. This grieved the devout man. He felt that he was failing in his duty to the Church. So one day, although by this time half the clan was grown up, he decided to make a last heroic effort. The children, on sighting him, fled to the hills, as was their wont. But the minister just knocked at the cottage door and went in, as if little concerned. With the shepherd and his wife he sat long in conversation—so long, indeed, that sheer curiosity enticed these wild things to come out of their hidie-holes, and creep silently round the doorstep. They were anxious to see what the stranger really looked like. As the minister heard the suppressed whisperings of the clan, now congregated outside the door, his eye alighted on a pail of water standing under the kitchen dresser. Picking it up noiselessly, he crept to the door, and, splashing its entire content over the scattering clan, he exclaimed: " Iain, Angus, Mairi, Seoras, Donald, Murdo, Kirsty, and the rest of you, I hereby baptize you all in the name of the Lord! "

* * * * *

In the playground of Boxer's school we indulged in all sorts of queer country games, many of which may be quite obsolete by now. The names of only two occur to me. One was known as ' In-and-out-the-Window ', and consisted of an elaborate jing-a-ring. The other was called ' Knifack '. This was played on short grass or hardened soil, and involved the placing of the point of a pocket-knife blade on various parts of one's clothing or anatomy, and then flicking it away in such a manner as to ensure that the blade stuck in the ground.

In this playground, too, the older boys used to repeat with relish all the bawdy songs and titbits they had picked up from their elders. Suggestive words, sung to well-known airs, were a peculiar feature of the countryside. The air known as *The Cock o' the North*, for instance, carried lines with which everyone, young and old alike, was familiar. Dare I repeat the first three lines, and leave the rest to memory?

Chase me, Charlie!
I've got barley
Up the leg o' ma draars!

* * * * *

In addition to the summer holidays, which extended over six weeks and not an hour longer, we were granted a day or two during the half-yearly Sacrament. Fast Day—a Thursday—was always a holiday, the argument being that, as most parents were fully occupied on that day in putting on their Sunday-bests and trudging miles from their crofts to one church or another, there was no time to prepare their offspring for school. Furthermore, while the parents were praying, the older children were obliged to stay at home to tend the croft. This entailed feeding the poultry, attending to the fire, cooking the dinner for the returning churchgoers, gathering sticks, bringing in water, herding the kye, looking after the babies. Sometimes the school buildings were requisitioned for public worship on such occasions. As at Applecross, however, Communion was often celebrated on the hillside, in the open. In a big tent erected near by, the communicants assembled in the event of rain. And what glorious capers we children had there before the service began, playing hide-and-seek, or see-sawing on the hard, wooden forms!

Gee Gee was ready to turn his hand to anything. When one of the local preachers fell ill, did he not take his place for six consecutive Sundays? "And all the people of the congregation said they would never forget his sermons," his youngest daughter recently assured me—a little ambiguously.

* * * * *

Severe and prolonged snowstorms were much more common in the Highlands then than they are nowadays. At times stretches of the road leading to the school at Gledfield lay under three or four feet of snow. I recall a wintry day when a girl living near by and myself were the only pupils who turned up, out of a roll of over a hundred. A further fall of snow eliminated the girl the following day; and for the remainder of the week I was the sole scholar to put in appearance. To a large extent this was attributable to the Colonel's insistence that his bairns should be hardy. The journey through the snow to school was facilitated by picking my way along the top of the dyke separating the road from fields, thus avoiding the deepest drifts.

On those very stormy days I was left alone to crouch over the schoolroom fire for a couple of hours. No member of the staff showed face at all. About noon Boxer, whose house adjoined the school, would wander along that dark, connecting passage to assure himself that teaching was out of the question. He would glance round the empty forms as a matter of routine, examine me on the part of the Shorter Catechism prescribed for that particular day, and then inform me that, having now complied with regulations so far as they affected the attendance roll, I was at liberty to find my way home as best I could. He did not even have the imagination to congratulate me on my intrepidity in coming a goodly step, day after day, often in a raging blizzard, when scholars living a stone's-throw away were absenting themselves.

As children in the Highlands, we trudged to school in all weathers. So far as mere attendance was concerned, climatic conditions affected us little. The first prize I ever received was for perfect attendance. The Colonel's comment on this was devastating. Anyone, he pointed out, could obtain a prize for regular attendance: a prize of that sort usually went to the child with no brains at all!

When, some years later, we went to school at Edinburgh, it appeared strange to us that, even taking into account the dreich and inclement winters often experienced in that city, any little thing provided our classmates with an excuse for absence. I now see that this was due to our totally different attitude to weather. As a family reared in the country, we regarded weather merely as an incident, although aware, of course, that the nature of it affected the country and country activities in a way it never could have affected the town. To us, the more boisterous the weather, the greater the inducement to be out in it. Who wanted to stay indoors when the snows lay thickly around us, or when a deluge brought spates to our rivers and floods to the low-lying places? Even at the Equinox we had to be out and about, battling against the gale in sheer ecstasy. At this season of the year we would walk miles to examine fallen timber, or to gaze at the roaring torrents that so often carried away both road and railway bridges in our own or a neighbouring parish.

CHAPTER VI

ANOTHER SCHOOL OR TWO

AS TIME wore on, my parents observed that I was assimilating rather much local colour; and so they decided to consign me to a fee-paying school, the tone and social standing of which were regarded as being superior.

I was now sent off to Tain Royal Academy, along with Jessie, my eldest sister. She and I were twin souls in those early days. We walked together; and we talked together. We wandered through the same woods, and lingered by the same shore-lands. We had the same friends, and visited them together. We now travelled to school by the same train and, at a later stage in our career, by the same horse-bus, when we could persuade the inn coachman to give us a lift on the long road to the last school we attended together. If late in arriving, we were arraigned simultaneously before the class to withstand the same ordeal. " Mine didn't hurt a bit! Did yours? " Jessie would ask me quite audibly before teacher and class, after each of us had received a 'pandy'.

We laughed together; and we cried together: we shared our delights and our sorrows. And, when the nursemaid once asked me at the age of eight whom I meant to marry when I grew up, I could think of no one as desirable as Jessie, and sobbed bitterly on having it explained that, for reasons of consanguinity, which I did not follow in the least, such a marriage was not permissible. In my dilemma, the only consolation came from Jessie herself. When asked whom *she* had thought of marrying, her one thought was of me! We felt that, if agreed upon this point, we might be able to defy those who conspired to separate us. The nursemaid, however, resorted to her

Bible to prove to us that such unions were both unlawful and contrary to ' The Word '. Against evidence so incontrovertible we were powerless.

In course of time Jessie's affection began to move in another direction. By the age of seven, she had fallen violently in love with Fergus MacLeod, the middle-aged nephew of the innkeeper at High Wind. She liked Fergus's neat moustache: its bristliness intrigued her when he kissed her. By the time she was eight, she had fallen with equal violence for a house-painter from Tain, who came to re-decorate our home, and remained with us for some weeks. He was about sixty-five, had long, drooping whiskers, was an elder in a kirk in Tain, and sang hymns very pleasantly when papering our nursery. Then she transferred her affections to John Bannerman, one of the railway porters at High Wind. John is now a senior official at Inverness station, complete with due proportion of gold braid. When I see him there about twice a year, his first enquiry is always for " little Jessie ".

* * * * *

Our attendance at Tain Royal Academy entailed a fourteen-mile journey by train about 7.30 each morning. Sometimes we had to dash off without any breakfast. The porridge was usually too hot. The maids had slept in; and so had we in consequence. Then, we were obliged to wander about the streets of Tain for a couple of hours, or about the playground, until the school-day opened with prayers at 10 a.m. This late hour was explained by the fact that many of the pupils had to come in from outlying districts. As the convenience of children was little considered in those days, they had to take advantage of whatever means of transport were available. Motor-cars were rare in rural Scotland, and bus services entirely unknown. The only part of the school accessible to the early comers was the entrance passage with the lockers containing the hockey-sticks. On frosty mornings an energetic game was the sole way we could keep warm.

There were also hours of dreary loitering at Tain in

the dark, winter evenings, waiting for the last northbound train, which was often two or three hours late, heavy snowstorms having held up the connection where the main line between Perth and Inverness traverses the Grampian wilds at the Pass of Drumuachdar. The evening train travelling north to Wick and Thurso was obliged, therefore, to defer its departure until the southern train arrived. Add to this the time lost in snowy weather between Inverness and Tain, and you have some idea of the hours that Jessie and I had to while away in prowling about Tain station. The generous waitingroom fire certainly did something to compensate for the exhaustion and waste of hours that we bairns ought to have been spending in sleep. We regarded it as a great mercy when the goods train came in first and got clear, since the compassionate guard used to take us home in his van, often an hour or two before we otherwise would have left Tain. We loved to crouch over the wee stove in the guard's van, and accept a warming mugful of his tea. This was in the days when guards and enginemen alike had to infuse their own tea during the journey, since thermos-flasks were unknown in the North, except when 'the gentry' arrived on The Twelfth to shoot anything that came their way. Sometimes the guard would take his teapot along to the front of the train, and hold it gingerly to a waste-pipe at the side of the engine, while the stoker from his cabin turned on a jet of scalding water.

As the days shortened, the lamps of the railway carriages were lit at Tain, on the platform of which station stood a lamp-room containing all manner of equipment now quite obsolete. This lamp-lighting necessitated a wait of a few extra minutes, to enable a porter to walk from one end of the train to the other, on the roof of the carriages, carrying a naphtha flare or torch of cotton-waste dipped in paraffin. With this he put a light to each lamp as he passed along. Additional delay was sometimes caused when a lamp refused to take the light, and another had to be brought from the lamp-room. When the days grew shorter still, the train arrived at Tain already lit up at some station farther south —at Dingwall or at Invergordon, perhaps.

Central heating was then as foreign to the Highland Railway as was electricity. Passengers in snowy weather sat muffled up in the compartments with their feet on those huge, flat foot-warmers provided by the Company in irregular numbers, and upon quite irregular occasions. These, too, are obsolete; but in those times there was always some congestion in the compartments containing them. My sister and I made a bee-line for them in order to melt the frozen snow off our boots. And sometimes (the little devils that we were!) the train was delayed for a moment or two while we dragged a couple of these ponderous things out of one compartment to another. With these extra ones we were able to produce the most glorious frowst!

The homeward journeys in the dark were often very trying, especially when a snow-plough had to be fixed in front of the engine. During the first part of the journey Jessie and I amused ourselves by counting the flashes from the lighthouse at Tarbat Ness, as the train swung round the shore of the Dornoch Firth between Tain and Edderton.

All the railway staff knew us intimately, since we were the only really young season-ticket holders on this line. But for the little attentions they showed us—the guard with the mug of hot tea; the drivers and stokers, who now and then lifted us up into the engine cabin for a wee warm; the porters who attended to the waitingroom fire for us, and often saw that we had a foot-warmer or two in our carriage—I doubt whether either of us could have endured the strain.

* * * * *

It was during my time at Tain Academy that I told my first major falsehood, and became conscious of my inclusion in The Fall, as depicted in Genesis; and for a while I endured corresponding pangs of remorse.

In the course of a particularly boring lesson I was enjoying a large piece of French nougat, when the teacher noticed the telltale bulge in my cheek, and accused me of the enormity of eating sweets in class. I pleaded surprise and innocence, and, even when ordered to spit out the offending lump in full view of the class, insisted that it was but a piece of paper. As a result of this brazen falsehood I was ' kept in ' after school, and nearly missed my train in consequence. For several days I was haunted by fear of expulsion; but my remorse was shortlived.

A classmate had formed the commendable habit of taking me home with him at the lunch interval. Anxious on my first visit to make the best possible impression on his mother, I embarked on a real whopper. I described how I amused myself at weekends with a homemade raft on the deep river meandering past our house. This so fired the boy's imagination that he repeated his invitations in the confident hope that he might share one of these weekends. Despite the fact that his mother was familiar with our district, and must have known that my river was nothing more than the ditch running by the fringe of the woods, I continued to embellish my story on each succeeding visit, until finally she denounced me as an incorrigible little liar, and no fit companion for her son. Thereafter I had to find my lunches elsewhere.

Those days at Tain were not entirely without lighter interludes, however. During the lunch interval one day, I accompanied some older boys to the sheriff court, where old Sandy MacLean, a crofter from a neighbouring village, was on trial for sheep-stealing, a crime that interested us immensely, since we believed it still was punishable by death. The case so fascinated us that, unmindful of school, we sat on to hear the result. Next morning, when we were assembled for prayers, the headmaster made very scathing reference (no names mentioned!) to certain boys who had neglected their studies to listen to sordid details about a wretched sheep-stealer. Though greatly embarrassed by this exposure of our unregeneracy, we had a secret feeling that this escapade had been well worth while. Had we not been privileged to witness the conclusion of the proceedings, and to hear the sheriff give judgment and pass sentence on poor Sandy? In our heart of hearts, however, we were a little disappointed he got no more than a few weeks' imprisonment, since we had looked forward with confidence to a sight of the ominous Black Cap.

The death-sentence for sheep-stealing, I believe, is still part of the penal code of Scotland.

* * * * *

Tain Royal Academy, by the way, has many distinguished former pupils. In the field of literature, moreover, the town has achieved prominence; and in this connection the name of Dr. Halliday Sutherland is perhaps outstanding. Halley (as he is called by those to whom he has endeared himself) had left Tain before I was old enough to go to school there. But I well remember his younger brother, Frank, though he was at the top of the school when I was still in the very junior department. Many old pupils must recall the occasion on which Frank—a genial, ginger-headed loon who, eventually, followed his father and brother into medicine—incurred the displeasure of the science master, who asked him why he had failed to carry out a certain scientific experiment according to instructions. Frank excused himself by remarking that the laboratory was not adequately equipped. Few school-boys in *those* days possessed such delightful self-assurance!

Of the Tain folk only a few stand out in my memory. I recall the kindnesses of Miss MacGill, our art mistress, who in recent years, as Mrs Helen Drever, has become so wellknown through her delightful children's books and her work with the B.B.C.

Then there was Sheriff and Mrs MacKenzie who, by virtue of his office, kept themselves somewhat aloof from the common herd, though "Mrs Sheriff" discharged her social obligations to the town by giving a large party now and then. There was much bragging among those school-children whose parents had been invited.

Another unforgettable character was the Rev. Mr Cameron, the long, lanky, frock-coated incumbent of St. Duthus Episcopal Church. He had a pronounced lisp, which, added to his affected Oxford accent, made him a ready subject for mimicry. Consequently, his parochial visits to Aunt Dorothy at Cnocnamoine were always a source of enjoyment. His son, Donald—a bonnie fechter—was in my class at the Academy; and there was seldom a scrap in the town in which Donald Cameron was not a participant. This reminds me that some years later, when I was home on leave, I encountered Mr Cameron on the platform at Tain, and congratulated him on a recent distinction which Donald had won in the navy. "Well, you thee, Alaththair, my thon, Donald, hath alwayth been a shyocking boy to fight. I thimply can't think where Donald got hith fighting inthinkth fwom. It thertainly wathent from me. It mutht have been from hith mothther!"

In a somewhat different category came Mr Alexander Munro, who placed the initials, M.A., after his name. His claim to them rested solely on his qualifications as a *M*anure *A*gent.

Then there was another member of that Rossshire clan called Willie Munro. He was inordinately ugly, and had a head so large that no hatter could fit him, which explained how he might be seen about the town in a big straw-hat belonging to his sister-in-law.

Willie was very cautious in the conduct of his love-affairs. He was aware of the Highland superstition that running water will check the career of a pursuing ghost, and believed further that it absolved him from any amorous obligations. He saw to it, therefore, when plighting his troth, as he frequently did, that a stream ran between him and the lady of his choice, thus protecting himself when the invariable complications arose.

* * * * *

One day in summer, when returning from Tain, the train halted for some unknown reason on the single track in the Gearrchoile Wood. As it seemed to be in no hurry to proceed to the platform a few hundred yards ahead, and our house was plainly visible from this part of the line, I decided to take a short-cut home. I flung my school-books out on to the embankment, and was on the point of leaping down to the track, when a school-girl in the compartment took fright at my escapade and slammed the carriage door, smashing the middle finger of my left hand. I ran home in a state of great pain and profuse bleeding. It looked as though amputation were inevitable; but my father administered chloroform and performed so successful an operation that my finger was saved. To-day, but for the suspicion of a stitch or two, it betrays no evidence of ever having been damaged—a wonderful tribute to the Colonel's skill.

With this accident terminated our connection with Tain Academy. Some weeks afterwards, when my finger was quite healed, Jessie and I were bundled off to the parish school over at Bonar-Bridge, in Sutherland. A two-mile tramp every morning and afternoon now took the place of the fourteen-mile train journey. Sometimes our presence on the road synchronised with the movements of MacPherson's horse-bus, plying regularly between the inn at Bonar-Bridge and the railway station at High Wind. When it contained no passengers—no commercial travellers, fishers of salmon, nor members of the 'gentry'—the driver usually gave us a lift. Frequently we just *took* one by scrambling on to the back step, unbeknown to him, and hanging on with grim determination. If he suspected this, the end of his whip would whizz round the corner as he drove on. The vehemence of that whip soon dislodged us; and great was our delight when he lashed away with no one there at all! I often had reason to remember the step of that bus when, as a school-boy at Edinburgh, I used to see the children riding gaily on the back axle of an old horse-cab, unknown to the dozing cabbie, while some jealous urchin standing by yelled to him "Slash ahint! Slash ahint!"

The most felicitous feature of this school at Bonar was that, at the close of each session, every pupil received the present of a book, thanks to some beneficent provision made by Andrew Carnegie, who resided for part of the year at his palatial Castle of Skibo, less than a dozen miles away. As a rule, the actual presentation was made by a member of the Carnegie family. These presents were not prizes in the strict sense, since efficiency was not taken into account in any way, which explains how nine-year-old Jessie was saddled with a copy of *Chambers's Twentieth Century Dictionary*, and why I was obliged to carry home a book that to me was valueless except as a reminder that, for the first time in my life, I had been awarded a gift through neither fault nor effort on my part.

Though this generous distribution has been discontinued, at the present time Mrs Carnegie, *in absentia*, entertains all the pupils to a social function held in the school at Christmas, when a present is handed to each by the factor for the Skibo Estates. Prizes for efficiency are now awarded at the close of the session. These are purchased with a fund supported by local subscriptions, to which Mrs Carnegie contributes handsomely. No attempt is now made to give each pupil a prize, except in the infant department.

Looking up the River Ness toward the Islands and the Great Glen. To the right may be seen St. Andrew's Cathedral, behind which rises the wooded outline of Tomnahurich

" I could have wept the first time I clambered on to the Cumberland Stone, and listened to my father's explanation of its name "

The Cumberland Stone, Culloden

Culloden Cottage, a relic of 'The Forty-five,' now preserved by the Gaelic Society of Inverness

CHAPTER VII

HIGHLAND HOLIDAY

A HIGH TIDE, moonlit, and ebbing swiftly and dangerously, carrying seaward with it an overloaded rowing-boat. Such is one of the most vivid recollections of what purported to be my first holiday in the accepted sense of the word. To a child at school, no holiday is worthy of the name that does not entail his being taken from home a respectable distance, and permitted to live there for not less than a week.

There came a summer when Mabel and the family entrained for Fortrose, the terminus of the Black Isle railway line, and established themselves for six weeks at a farm overlooking the Beauly Firth, the hills of Nairn, and the narrows where Chanonry Point juts out toward Fort George. The farm was tenanted by people called Munro. It lay in the very heart of the farmlands of the Black Isle (that Isle that isn't an isle!), and was called Mount Pleasant. The farmhouse faced south. Perched on the crest of a long, steep field, and backed by a clump of trees, it was surrounded by much of the most fertile land in Scotland. The Black Isle is famed for its farms. It is, indeed, one of our most bountiful granaries.

Old Munro, unlike Old King Cole, was a grumpy old soul. His attitude to life in general seemed to have been produced by the combined efforts of a natural ugliness, an unhealthy nose, an impediment in his speech, and a generous touch of asthma. He always appeared to be keeping a watchful eye on us, lest we should stray among such preserves as were definitely *not* included among the amenities for which Mabel was paying. He scrupulously guarded the gooseberry bushes in his garden, for instance.

The financial arrangement between the Munroes and Mabel did not entitle us to one gooseberry, although, as a family, we would have preferred a few minutes' freedom among those laden bushes to all his home-killed meat. A high wall, a railing, a closed gate, and the baleful eye of Mr Munro all conspired to prevent us from getting anywhere near this forbidden fruit.

Mrs Munro, likewise, exercised a restraining influence. We rather regarded her as a replica of Queen Victoria, so similar did she appear, particularly in the matter of dress and head-gear, to those pictures of the Queen given away with periodicals early in the century, and framed by her patriotic subjects. When seated by the fire in her upholstered chair, her walking-stick by her side, she was indeed a rural edition of the good Queen. This resemblance was even more striking on Sundays, when she donned a specially embroidered lace cap. She was the business manager of the establishment, and knew both sides of the smallest coin. To this day I visualise her as she came out of the garden, holding a bowl-ful of rasps in one hand, and sedulously pulling-to the gate with the other in a way that conjured up in our young minds the Garden of Eden. In one important essential, however, the garden at Mount Pleasant differed from the Garden of Eden, in that *all* of it was out of bounds to us.

* * * * *

The farm included an inordinate flock of poultry, ranging from the merest chicks to peacocks and veteran bubbly-jocks. Among the firs flanking the farmhouse on the west, guinea-fowls—the first I had ever seen—uttered their shrill calls at eerie intervals during the night. Some distance behind the farm, and on the spine of the Black Isle, a sawmill spent the long days of summer in dealing with the trees then being cleared from the extensive pinewoods around it. The lumbermen lived in bothies amid a sea of saw-dust and discarded bark; and I found immense delight in visiting them in the early evening, when they were preparing their meal in sooty and dented utensils. With my love for machinery, I found the engine and furnace of this sawmill particularly alluring. I soon made friends with the engine-man. Under his supervision he allowed me to fling untrimmed timber into the furnace to maintain the requisite pressure of steam for the driving of the saws. Sometimes he even encouraged me to handle the appropriate wheels and levers when, at the end of the day's operations, it was necessary to shut off steam, and bank down the fire. Small wonder I wanted to be an engine-man when I grew up!

Much of this holiday was spent on the sands with pail and spade, either at Fortrose or at Rosemarkie; and I well remember my distress when an exceptionally high tide washed away the foundations of a sand-castle upon which I had laboured for several days. When tired of paddling or of castle-building, we sallied forth to gather white rasps growing in wild profusion by the wayside, not far from the farm.

Another of our haunts was the Faery Glen at Rosemarkie. There we often looked for evidence of the Little Folk, and watched for the rings spun by louping trout in the Faery Pool. There, too, we marvelled at the steep sand-cliffs, so honeycombed with the burrows of swift and swallow.

But what fascinated us most of all was the little, wooden structure set down in a copse of whin and birch and broom at the foot of the brae, and to which Jessie and I gave the name of Jack-and-Jill's House. Its sides were of wood, painted in bright green, contrasting almost as sharply with its surroundings as did the bright red of its roof. To us it was strictly out of bounds, which greatly enhanced its interest, already whetted by the rumour of a ghost. The proximity of the local volunteers' rifle-range, we afterwards learnt, was the real reason for the restriction.

Motor-cars were quite a novelty on the Black Isle then. Our journeys furth of Mount Pleasant, therefore, had to be made by trap. When the fish-wife came up the hill with her creel, and induced Mabel to conduct the family over to see her at the fishing village of Avoch (pronounced *Auch*), we all set out in the Munroes' trap. So many of us had to be accommodated, somehow or other, in this old-fashioned vehicle, that the expedition was one calculated to place a good deal of strain on the pony by the time the poor creature brought us all home again in the evening. But those visits to Avoch have left memories of the geranium flowering in the fish-wife's window, of the whitings and speldings and smokies she gave us for tea, and of the excellent girdle-scones she baked on our arrival.

* * * * *

The Munroes had been in the habit of entering half a dozen animals for the annual horse-show held on the edge of the whin moor, that flat expanse lying between the barracks at Fort George and the neighbouring village of Campbeltown, or Ardersier. And each year their exhibits gained prizes, as was manifest from the number of multi-coloured cards tacked on to the posts in the large stable. In places, the rafters and uprights were quite hidden by these cards.

Similarly decorated was the byre, since the Mount Pleasant cows had also been prize-winners from time to time. In that byre I had my first lesson in milking. I sat on a three-legged stool, while Chrissie Munro, daughter and dairymaid, tried to teach me. But my clumsiness so exasperated the cow, otherwise a docile creature, that she swished her tail impatiently, stamped her hooves, and finally gave a kick that couped me and the milk-pail into the gutter. My attempts at milking were never too successful, though a few years later, under Aunt Dorothy's tuition, I learnt how to milk her goats. But what I did enjoy about Mount Pleasant was carrying to each beast an armful of hay after dark, when the byre was illumined by the dingy light of an old-fashioned lantern hanging from a nail. Nowadays, of course, up-to-date byres, even in the Highlands, are lit by electricity. I was rather small to be able to get each cow's ration into her rack without spilling a little of it; and this used to make Mr Munro very wild indeed. Nevertheless, I went on trying, evening after evening, until eventually I became adept. Whenever I heard the rattle of lanterns and milk-pails by the scullery door, out I rushed to the byre as though I, too, were obliged to do my share of this routine work.

The opening of the byre door was a signal to the cows that milking- and feeding-time had arrived. The first fork-load of hay always occasioned a mild stampede. Tails swished vigorously: chains rattled: hooves stamped: inquisitive eyes appeared over each partition: distended nostrils gave forth clouds of warm vapour in the lantern-light.

* * * * *

Not long after the family's installation at Mount Pleasant, the horse-show was due to take place. On the day preceding it, the animals entered for exhibition left in the care of various farm-workers, for, although Fort George and Fortrose lie so close to one another in terms of bee-flight—separated merely by the narrows of the Beauly Firth at Chanonry—the journey by road is very round-about. One has to traverse most of the Black Isle by a secondary road to join the main Highland highway at the Muir of Ord, and then travel round the head of the firth, and well beyond Inverness, before branching eastward for Ardersier and the Fort. I cannot quite remember whether it was possible to transport the larger live-stock across the Kessock Ferry, the readiest means of communication between the Black Isle and Inverness, thus dispensing with the much longer journey by the Muir of Ord. But I do know that the ferrying of animals across the Chanonry narrows has never been very practicable. A moment's glance at a map of this area will illustrate how circuitous is the journey by road necessitated by the penetration of the firth at this point.

Early on the day of the show, we all went down to Fortrose to be ferried across to Fort George, that huge pile of red sandstone so wellknown to those connected with our Highland regiments.

Various distractions, not least among them the local pubs, supplemented by the bottle in the hip pocket, prevented our re-embarking for several hours after the conclusion of the horse-show. Although the methodical Mabel had assembled us all by the shore at sundown, it was some considerable time before our hired boatmen, now well soaked in liquor, put in an appearance, and in drunken fashion essayed to row us home. A high tide was now ebbing rapidly, carrying us out to the open waters of the Moray Firth. The boatmen, every moment becoming more langorous at the oars, were finding it increasingly difficult to bring us ashore by the old pier at Fortrose. Schools of porpoises birled past us, breaking the surface of the moonlit tide with their fins. I tried hard to concentrate on their movements, in order to distract my mind from a situation that every second was growing more and more menacing. But, when our tipsy navigators almost capsized the craft amid the swirling currents, even the stoicism of Mabel was insufficient to restrain me from shrieking in terror. Had it not been for the timely assistance of some men from a small sailing-ship lying at anchor off the pier, we all might have been drowned. My cries had attracted their attention; and in no time they were rowing strongly to our rescue across the moonlit ebb.

CHAPTER VIII

MY FIRST TOWN

OH! THE joy of those first weeks in Inverness, that exquisite, little town "placed by the shore of one of the loveliest estuaries in the world," as Ruskin wrote—"placed between the crests of the Grampians and the flowing of the Moray Firth, as if it were a jewel clasping the folds of the mountains to the blue zone of the sea."

Thither the Colonel removed the family, preparatory to its final anchorage at Edinburgh. We had been accustomed to one or two of the smaller towns of the Highlands before this, however—to Tain, Invergordon, Dingwall, and Dornoch, for example—and had even paid short visits to Inverness, when Mabel took us to the photographer's, and returned home with us by train at the end of the day. But Inverness was the first town in the proper sense in which we ever really lived.

Within a month or so of our arrival, the Colonel, addicted as ever to interminable walks, had introduced me to everything of interest within a radius of ten miles. Drummossie Muir—Culloden—attracted us almost every Saturday. On our way there, we always halted in the village of Culcabock to look at King Duncan's Well, and at the stone in the wall reputed to mark his grave. The Islands or, perhaps, Tomnahurich saw us on Sunday afternoons, after Sunday-school. Often he accompanied Iain and me down to the Kessock Ferry, where one could cross to the Black Isle in the matter of a few minutes.

The funny, little streets of Inverness itself we came to love. They were tremendous in comparison with what we had been used to. The High Street of Tain, every nook of which Jessie and I knew, was now quite dwarfed by the High Street of Inverness. The horse-cabs delighted us; and we thought it grand that we could run as quickly as the cabbies could drive along its cobble-stoned thoroughfares. There were no taxi-cabs in the North as yet.

The Town Clock and the bells in the tall steeple at the corner of Church Street and Bridge Street fascinated us, and increasingly so when the Colonel told us that, nearly a hundred years before, an earthquake shock had so twisted the spire of the steeple that it took several years to get it straight again. It was in this connection that I first heard the name of Hugh Miller, since our father, anxious at all times to improve the shining hour where knowledge and education were concerned, seized upon my interest in the earthquake as an opportunity for introducing me to *My Schools and Schoolmasters*, wherein Hugh Miller records his disapproval of the repairs then being carried out on the town steeple.

Then there was that lovely structure by the river's bank —St. Andrew's Cathedral, the most imposing ecclesiastical edifice in the town, though of no great age. This place of worship of the Scottish Episcopal Church, built as recently as 1867, was an especial curiosity to us as Presbyterian children, in that one could enter and leave it without let or hindrance at any time of the day, and any day of the week. This we thought very extraordinary. All the churches with which we had been familiar hitherto were locked away after evening service on Sunday, and not unlocked again until the forenoon of the following Sunday. To us it was nothing short of mysterious that one could wander in and out of St. Andrew's at will. And, when we discovered that different parts of its interior had specific names attached to them—nave, aisles, transepts, chancel—we became very suspicious that the work of John Calvin and of John Knox was being undermined, and had to consult the Colonel very earnestly on this point! To our young, Presbyterian minds, the existence in Inverness of a Cathedral, so replete with stained-glass windows, savoured of idolatry!

As I grew up, however, I began to realise how incomplete this lovely, Highland town would be without St. Andrew's. One appreciates this when lingering on the Castle Hill at dusk and sundown, gazing up-river, while the sleepy town, quiescent in a haze of blue smoke from evening fires, is momentarily stirred by the peal of the Cathedral's bells.

* * * * *

The shops of Inverness we loved as children, particularly those situated in the rectangle formed by High Street, Church Street, Union Street, and Academy Street. Then there was an ice-cream shop in Queensgate that lured us with our sparse coppers, and another in Bridge Street where, even for a ha'penny, one could purchase quite a respectable slider. And I remember a wee shop in Castle Street where we could buy a fist-ful of home-made toffee for a penny, or a dozen of those big "doddles" known as Berwick Cockles.

But the greatest attraction of all was the sixpence-ha'penny bazaar, which had just opened in the town. In order to purchase some particularly appealing object there, we used to save up our pennies with fanatical fervour, denying ourselves all sorts of minor pleasures in the process.

The shops were so numerous and so fine, especially those trading in antiques and souvenirs. The fruiterers' establishments held us spellbound, though we seldom could afford anything but the most ordinary of their wares. But two bananas for a penny, or half a pound of white grapes for half as much again, we regarded as quite a generous exchange. I smell even yet those shops of early days in Inverness. They had the clean and pure scent one gets on opening a box of rosy apples. And I also smell in imagination the briny fish-stalls in the covered-in market, with its four entrances, in and out of which the Colonel used to wander of an evening, in the hope of collecting his errant flock for family-worship, an institution that endured with the utmost regularity in our household until the Great War broke things up—broke up the personnel of the home and, perhaps, to some extent, the orthodox inclinations of many of us who returned from it.

There was one building in Inverness that, for a day or two once a year, held our particular attention. This was the Northern Meeting Rooms, situated near the top of Church Street. Annually, in the third week of September, two famous balls are held here. The Meeting was instituted as long ago as 1788, and is still regarded in the North as a social event of some importance. The forenoons are reserved for Highland Games, which are held in the Northern Meeting Park, on the other side of the river, while the evenings are devoted to Highland Balls. Free of our mother's restraining influence at this time, we used to stand outside the Rooms among the crowd assembled there to see ' the gentry ' arrive in all its finery.

As for the railway-station, never had we seen so many trains coming and going at the same time. It was thrilling to stand by any one of its terminal platforms to watch all those people getting in or out of railway-carriages. The penny-in-the-slot machines captivated us. Although, at the price, we could have purchased in any one of the town's sweetie-shops something more delectable than the contents of those wee packets, the experience of automatically making one's purchases in this way more than compensated for the inferiority of the articles obtained. We did not mind how viscous was the toffee, nor how stale the chocolate, these machines supplied. And you can imagine the disappointment when, having carelessly placed our coin in the wrong slot, we pulled out a box of Swan Vestas instead of something edible!

Then, there was the machine enticing you to try your strength, and bearing the prominent legend " Moderate strength rings the bell: Great strength returns the penny." This challenge to prowess readily deprived us of the few coppers we could afford; but we were anxious to compete with the powerful railway porters whom we had seen inserting pennies so casually from time to time, never failing to retrieve them. The advice on the machine that, only by the single grip of one hand, could the return of the penny be ensured, was just so much mechanical nonsense, designed to effect the maximum number of failures.

The nooks and corners of that same station became unusually familiar to us when we made friends with some other urchins, and played hide-and-seek in and about this pretty, little town. These urchins listened with amazement as Iain and I told them of our former home some sixty miles away, for they regarded anything farther north than Inverness as *terra incognita.*

For many months I found Inverness a great diversion. Each day produced some fresh attraction. First and foremost of these was the Castle; and the various corners of the Castle Hill provided a playground, the like of which we had not known. We had never seen a castle quite like this. With the exception of Dunrobin, our Highland castles hitherto had been in ruins—Eilean Donan and Ardvreck, for instance, and Castle Maol, overlooking the narrows at Kyleakin. (Skibo the Colonel never allowed us to regard as a castle in the true sense.) But here, in Inverness, was a fine building of red sandstone, castellated in Tudor style, and in perfect repair, inhabited, during the daytime at any rate, by those engaged in the multifarious county offices housed therein. But we were a little disappointed to discover that all the cannons set around it in positions of defence were mere dummies.

What diverted me more than anything was the old well of the original stronghold, laid bare by a subsidence in the ground about the time of our arrival in Inverness in 1909. The well was being cleared out by workmen, whose activities I watched with feverish excitement, especially after I had heard that water actually existed at a depth of nearly fifty feet.

* * * * *

To our sojourn in Inverness I owe my interest in matters

relating to the Stuarts. And how could it have been otherwise? The Colonel had given me some elementary instruction in the town's associations with King Brude in ancient times, with Macbeth and with William the Lion at a later date, and with Cromwell in the seventeenth century. Though these names conveyed little to me, anything connected with Prince Charlie or Flora MacDonald was vital, living, all-absorbing; and in learning about them afresh in this setting I felt as though the tragedy of Culloden had happened but a day or two before. When I wandered into the little museum, just by the public library yonder, and saw with my very own eyes some Jacobite relics, I would not have been the least surprised to hear that Prince Charlie was about to make a triumphal entry into the town. The tailors' establishments dotted about its shopping centre, displaying so conspicuously the tartans of the clans, certainly strengthened such a possibility in one's imagination. About the streets of Inverness one always sees a few men clad in the kilt, and women in tartan skirts. But, despite this gaiety, the air is strangely tinged at times with the pain of Culloden, though nearly two hundred years have passed since the clans were vanquished there.

Incidentally, any reference to King James and to Prince Charlie as the Old and Young *Pretender* was discouraged in our home. Though these terms occurred even in our history books, we were taught to regard them as unjustifiable and unchivalrous. It was fitting that we should speak of this hapless father and son as the Old and the Young *Chevalier*. Whatever shortcomings they may have had, there was no *pretence* about their claim. Our father's pronouncement on such matters carried more conviction than any printed word.

It was left to the Colonel to introduce us to the memorial to Flora MacDonald. Flora stood high among his heroines; and it was with a sense of duty to a lost cause, therefore, that he led Iain and me up to the Castle Hill one Saturday morning, that we might gaze with reverence on the bronze statue erected to her on the esplanade. He made us stand to attention, as he re-told how Flora effected Prince Charlie's escape. " What is she supposed to be looking for, father? " asked the intelligent Iain, having noticed that the statue shows Flora with her right hand shading her eyes, gazing away in the direction of the Great Glen of Scotland—watching intently, as our father now explained, for the arrival of the Highland clans from the west. Those clans might have saved poor Charlie from the final disaster that overwhelmed him and his cause at Culloden, but a few miles away, had they not been so disunited and so badly organised, and had some of them not tarried so long in coming to his aid.

I remember vividly how Iain and I stood by in wonderment while our father read aloud, in solemn tones, the Gaelic sentence on that memorial, and also Dr. Johnson's oft-quoted words—" The preserver of Prince Charles Edward Stuart will be mentioned in history, and, if courage and fidelity be virtues, mentioned with honour."

We were spellbound as he proceeded with his narrative. Every now and then, we turned our gaze in the airt of the Great Glen, hoping that, perhaps, even yet, the clans might have approached in sufficient numbers and panoply to have saved Charlie and the Jacobites from their final catastrophe, and thus ensured the recovery of an ancient crown lost to the Stuarts by the imprudence of their ancestors. Since the Colonel was a Jacobite at heart (and what Highlander is not?), he certainly filled us in those few minutes with the desire to know something of ' The Fifteen' and 'The Forty-five', and to visit such scenes associated with these luckless enterprises as now lay within reasonable reach. And this explains how Drummossie Muir—Culloden—became one of our favourite haunts.

Our visits to the Field of Culloden were innumerable. These were accomplished as a rule on foot, though a tardy train might have deposited us at Culloden Moor Station, roughly within a mile of the battlefield. In the summer and autumn months, fours-in-hand and even sixes-in-hand plied between the Station Square and the Cairn erected on the battlefield in 1881 by Duncan Forbes, the last resident proprietor of Culloden. To-day, these horse-coaches have been replaced by speedy charabancs. In any case, the Colonel believed that a good walk was the best thing in the world for a growing boy, as well as for himself. As the edge of the actual battlefield is some five miles from the town, our journeys in this airt seldom entailed a tramp of less than a dozen miles. Despite my training at Applecross, I sometimes found this a little tedious, and often affected fatigue in the hope of our taking the train on the homeward journey. But such trains as halted at Culloden Moor Station were so infrequent that the Colonel was always at an advantage when he parried my naïvety by observing that we could reach Inverness on foot long before a train was due at Culloden. In reflecting upon those days, I feel quite happy that our excursions were made on foot, and in conformity with his desire, since I am sure they instilled in me a love for this countryside, and a familiarity with it that has been most satisfying in later life.

The inscription on the principal cairn I read and re-read. For me it had an alluring charm. The cairn itself enshrined something far more telling than the mere site of the last battle contested on British soil. It epitomised the end of an old order of things, and the death of chivalry as Scotland had known it. That inscription I have read many times since those days; and it still has a wistful poignancy for me:

THE BATTLE OF CULLODEN

was fought on this moor

16th April, 1746

The Graves of the Gallant Highlanders
who fought for

SCOTLAND AND PRINCE CHARLIE

are marked by the names of their clans.

I could have wept, the first time I clambered on to that massive boulder, the Cumberland Stone, and listened to my father's explanation of its name. With the details of the battle I will not weary you. Suffice it to say that on this very moor was enacted a scene that, had fortune favoured otherwise, undoubtedly would have altered the entire course of British History, and possibly that of the world. In less than an hour the long struggle between Jacobite and Hanoverian was settled in the decisive rout of the former. The Red Coats' casualties were negligible. Those who lost their lives were buried near by, in the patch of arable ground that ever since has been termed the Field of the English. The vanquished Highlanders—and there were many of them—were buried on the field of battle, according to their clans, just where they fell. By the Well of the Dead stands a solitary stone marking the spot where the Chief of the MacGillivrays fell. Another stone near at hand commemorates fallen MacLeans, MacLachlans, and Atholl Highlanders. The Camerons, MacKintoshes, Stewarts of Appin, Frasers, and Campbells have head-stones of their own; and there are three stones defining the burial-place of the mixed clans.

CHAPTER IX

MORE OF INVERNESS

WITH INVERNESS are associated my earliest experiences with a bicycle. The Colonel had been one of the first in the Highlands to dispense with the ancient penny-farthing type. He resorted to cycling for sheer recreation and the joy of getting over the country independently and cheaply. Motor vehicles at that time were raucous and fumiferous, and our Highland roads little better than cart-tracks. The Colonel's bicycle, if seen alongside a modern model, would look hopelessly primitive. Even in those days we children criticized it, comparing it unfavourably with the newer models we used to examine so covetously in the shop windows of Inverness. Yet, he was proud of his 'machine'; and it always gave him great pleasure to regard himself as one of the pioneers of the 'Safety' bicycle.

One day our sister, Jessie, espied in the wee window of a wee bicycle shop in Baron Taylor's Lane a wee bicycle she thought she would like. As our father never could refuse Jessie anything, and Jessie was not altogether unaware of this, he purchased this wee bicycle for her. Having been utterly devoid of any business sense throughout the greater part of his life, he paid exorbitantly for it, and even gave his own bicycle in part payment. From a financial point of view, this transaction was a palpable swindle, as he himself realized a day or two later: adjudged solely by the amount of joy it brought us, it was supremely satisfactory. On it the entire family learned to ride. We were now most popular among the children of Inverness.

But to the adult population and the civic authorities we became the most infernal nuisance, flying downhill and round corners, our red kilts streaming behind us. When summer drought reduced the level of the River Ness to a few inches, and often left half its normal channel a dry ridge of pebbles, we delighted in cycling across the river's bed, in preference to using the bridges. But the fun of this was negligible as compared with that derived from pedalling furiously over the suspension-bridge up near the Infirmary. Two of us used to stand in the centre of this bridge and jump up and down in synchrony, until it swung beneath us and sent undulations of motion along from one end to another. When these were at their maximum, the third member of the family would cycle across at break-neck speed—if there happened to be no policeman in sight. It would be impossible to compute the number of times we were 'warned off' by the Inverness police when they caught us at our capers with that little bicycle.

One afternoon, as I came charging down Bank Street, Jessie rushed out to stop me, for she felt that I had had more than my fair share of the bicycle that day. That impulse on Jessie's part nearly cost me my life. I lost control, dashed into the railings at the foot, and somersaulted into the river below. Fortunately, the river carried a goodly volume of water at the time; and by some miracle I managed to scramble back to dry land, unscathed. The bicycle, meanwhile, was impaled on the railings; and our long-suffering father had to find quite a sum to have it repaired. That was the last occasion on which I cycled down Bank Street. Thereafter I resorted to the public park on the other side of the town, and tore round and round it very much in the spirit of the modern dirt-track fiend.

* * * * *

During the family's sojourn in Inverness, I was enrolled at yet another school. This was my fourth in a few years; and I now began to realise that, with each change of school, I was being thrust back a standard or two, and that it looked as though another change would precipitate me into the infant-room once more! My recollections of school at Inverness are extraordinarily vague. In no way was this due to waning enthusiasm on our father's part for the continuity of his offsprings' education. On the contrary, he always tried to arrange domestic matters so as to ensure that, if we left one school on a Wednesday, we went to our next the following day. But by this time we had an inkling that school at Inverness was merely a stop-gap, preliminary to our removal to Edinburgh, where he hoped the education of his children would begin in real earnest.

One of the most vivid recollections I have of this last school in the Highlands is my frantic hurrying up Stephen's Brae o' mornings, to avoid the corporal consequences of unpunctuality, trying to memorise on the way those doleful lines on the Inchcape Rock. Why on earth Ralph the Rover could not have left the bell where it was, I never could understand. His insistence on removing it was *my* undoing, as well as his. As for the Abbot of Aberbrothock, I was never able to twist either my tongue or my slate-pencil round his name.

The school-day began with Scripture. This involved our learning by heart certain selected passages from the New Testament. Ability to recite the thirteenth chapter of First Corinthians was the hall-mark of piety and diligence. And this reminds me that I was always a little intrigued by the idea of seeing through a glass darkly, associating it with an occasion when we watched an eclipse of the sun through a glass smoked over an oil lamp.

Twice or thrice weekly, immediately after the Scripture lesson, we had a crude form of mass singing under the direction of the late William Stewart Roddie, a professional singing teacher with white, patriarchal locks, who was Precentor at the High Church. Mr Roddie's didactic aspirations certainly transcended the *Rule, Britannia* category. He was more prone to the teaching of songs with pastoral settings—songs about frolicking lambkins and bright-eyed daisies. Nevertheless, I remember how, *ad nauseam*, he trailed us through *The Bonnie Woods o' Craigielea.* Those were the most monotonous woods I ever entered!

Mr Roddie's son, Willie, once conducted an Academy of Music in Church Street. There he taught me to play my first elementary melody by rolling my knuckles upon the black notes of the piano, and putting in an odd single note here and there to give some semblance of musical form.

As a boy of nine, I revelled in the tea-parties Willie used to arrange for the two of us in a cosy, little room in his Academy. He always provided me with a macaroon on these occasions, and a plateful of doughnuts. As there was a bitter feud between the Colonel and the Roddies (they were Mabel's friends!!), I was obliged to keep these tea-parties very secret. Likewise my visits to the Roddies' home at Woodlands, away up by the Islands. Two things about Woodlands I remember clearly. One was my first acquaintance with asbestos, since there was a gas-stove in the hall. The other was the strings of coloured beads dependent in the hall as a window-curtain. Never before had I seen beads put to so quaint a use. Jessie had had many a trayful of beads; but she never made anything so queer as a window-curtain out of them.

The elementary instruction in music—voice production from the father during school hours: knuckle technique from the son at tea-time—recalls that it was during our stay in Inverness I first heard a band, and a German band at that. These were the first Germans I had ever seen. Queer mortals I thought them. And, yet, were they so different from ourselves? This would be somewhere about 1908 or 1909, when one or two German bands were still wandering through the towns and larger villages of the Highlands. It was whispered even then that these bandsmen were in reality spies in the services of the Kaiser, secretly obtaining information about our naval base at Invergordon, in view of the Great War then approaching.

* * * * *

The River Ness, flowing broadly through the centre of the town, with the salt waters of the Beauly Firth not far off, and those lovely islands situated in the river about a mile from the Exchange, all combined to make Inverness a delectable playground. Invernessians have always been very proud of their Islands, laid out with walks and seats, and connected by foot-bridges. These sylvan retreats were especially enticing after dusk on a summer's evening, festooned with faery lights of many colours, a band accentuating the gaiety of the crowds promenading about them.

Alluring as I found the Islands, more alluring still were the locks at the Muirtown end of the Caledonian Canal. The pre-war traffic between the wharf at Muirtown and the centre of Inverness was enormous during the summer and autumn months. Every day in the season, excepting Sundays, scores of horse-drawn vehicles met the paddle-steamers sailing up through the Great Glen from the Fort-William end of the canal, so that the road between Muirtown and Inverness often resembled a Glasgow thoroughfare after a cup-tie final. The actual locks were busiest, of course, when the bulk of the Scottish Herring Fleet, consisting of some hundreds of wherries and drifters, passed through them on their way from the West Coast fishings to the East, or in the opposite direction, according to the time of year. But for the canal, they would have been obliged to sail round the north of Scotland and through the Pentland Firth.

One sunny forenoon my father and I arrived at Muirtown, when everything was quiet and peaceful. To the seaward lay a few boats, waiting to come inland: to the landward others hugged the banks of the canal, preparatory to moving seaward. To arrive at the Muirtown wharf, just as the requirements of a boat necessitated the opening of the lock gates, was my idea of bliss. But the lock-keepers seemed to be making no move on this occasion. Puzzled by this inactivity, I peered over the edge of one of the basins to find a couple of men slowly turning a wheel set up in the centre of a flat-bottomed coble, over the side of which hung a rope-ladder and a length of rubber tubing. Then I noticed strings of bubbles coming up to the surface, close to the lock-gates.

"There's a diver down there, Alasdair," my father remarked. "These men are pumping down air to him." I was thrilled. We waited until some cryptic signal passed between the men turning the wheel and the diver cleaning the bottom of the lock-gates, many feet below. Suddenly, the rope-ladder began to wriggle, as though someone out of sight were tugging at it. A minute or so later I could see a huge ball of shining copper slowly coming to the surface. Shall I ever forget my amazement when, eventually, a monstrous figure emerged, heavily encased as in impenetrable armour, and was helped into the coble? There he slumped on a thwart, as if dead, while the two men proceeded to unscrew his ponderous head-piece. The marvel of that spectacle stifled in me forever the ambition to be an engine-driver. I was determined now to be a diver, employed in cleaning the lock-gates of the Caledonian Canal.

Another haunt of boyhood might be mentioned in passing, because of its interest to folklorists—Tomnahurich, Inverness's burial-place, that densely wooded hill lying roughly a mile from the town, and at a distance resembling a prodigious up-turned boat. Philologists differ as to the origin of the name, of course, since philology can be a very inexact science. But there is ground for the view that Tomnahurich is derived from the Gaelic signifying 'Hill of the Faeries'.

The faery-lore of Tomnahurich is extensive. The

interior of the hill is regarded as a faery dwelling, with its door obscured from the eyes of ordinary mortals. We frequently heard tales of children who had been carried away by the faeries of Tomnahurich, and of unwary grown-ups who were encouraged to take part in the faery dance, thus forfeiting their freedom for a year and a day. And there was the case of John Fraser, the miller who, at a time when the faeries were responsible for a milk shortage, observed an agéd and odd-looking man emerge from Tomnahurich, carrying a hawthorn sapling. With commendable presence of mind, the miller broke the faery spell by giving the sapling a gash with his knife, whereupon a stream of milk poured from it.

In Tomnahurich, too, resides Thomas the Rhymer, who sought sanctuary there, in faery-land, where he will remain until Easter Friday and Shrove Tuesday exchange places on the Calendar. With Thomas the Rhymer—True Thomas, as he sometimes is called—were associated Thomas Cumming and Farquhar Grant, two Strathspey street-players, whom he engaged to supply the music for the faeries' dance inside Tomnahurich. They travelled from Strathspey to fulfil their engagement, crossing the River Ness by ferryboat. But just imagine their consternation when, as they returned home on what they thought was the following morning, they noticed a substantial stone bridge by which they might have crossed the previous evening! Furthermore, they could not understand why the Inverness folk had altered their attire so completely overnight, and were inclined to stand and stare and laugh at them, as they passed homeward through the town. They had been playing for the faeries in Tomnahurich for exactly a century, and had not known it!

* * * * *

The first big funeral I ever saw was to the cemetery at Tomnahurich. Indeed, it was the largest assemblage of human beings I had witnessed up to that time. Colonel —— had died; and, since he was being given a military funeral, and the Highlanders simply revel in anything of that nature, Inverness was veritably *en fête*. All the shops were closed in deference to the deceased, who was a person of some local importance. But he wasn't a *real* colonel, our father explained: he was only in the Territorials! Yet, I remember so vividly the coffin draped with the Union Jack, borne on a gun-carriage, preceded by pipers playing *The Flowers o' the Forest*, and followed by an interminable throng of serious-looking townspeople. The procession seemed an endless one, as it slowly wended its way toward the Hill of the Faeries. The entire population of the town was out that afternoon. Such inhabitants as were not lining the pavements, joined in the procession, at the tail-end of which followed scores of children, most of them barefooted, who had just tacked themselves on at the rear, regardless of official efforts to shoo them away. "O, King of Virtues! What a lot of people!" I thought, as I, too, fell in at the tail-end. Out to Tomnahurich we children all marched, affecting such semblance of solemnity as we could muster for the passing of a man about whom we knew absolutely nothing. Imagine our disappointment when, on reaching the gates of Tomnahurich, the undertakers and cemetery officials segregated us from the adult mourners, and chased us away! We felt we had been denied the best of the fun. In disconsolate mood, we hung about those gates until the whole show was over, and then raced back to the centre of the town.

* * * * *

Notwithstanding all these pranks, some of my memories of Inverness are not too happy. By this time, a rift in the matrimonial lute, due entirely to disparity in age and incompatibility of temperament, had so widened that the Colonel and Mabel now viewed one another with open hostility, regardless, it would seem, of the effect this was bound to have upon their young and sensitive offspring. On that very sad phase of my life I do not want to dwell unduly. But one incident relating to my parents' differences might be told appropriately here, since it happened in Inverness, and I am now old enough to see the absurd, as well as the tragic, side of it.

You must bear in mind that the Colonel's reverence for the Clan Gregor amounted to an obsession. Reluctance to share this passion constituted an offence more heinous than the seven deadly sins.

Our lovely mother was now living in the Queensgate Hotel, opposite the General Post-office, yonder, while my brother and sisters and I—five of us in all—resided with the Colonel not very far off, pending some re-arrangement in domestic affairs. One morning, to our dismay, he 'ordered' us—nay, *commanded* us—to be ready to proceed with him, *en masse*, to a destination not disclosed. We were duly paraded at the front door. Accompanied by the nurse, who looked after the two youngest members of the family, he led us off to the Queensgate, marched us upstairs and into the drawingroom in semi-military fashion, and halted us in the centre of the floor. The room was occupied for the most part by elderly ladies in the throes of knitting or crocheting, or of letter-writing at small tables placed here and there about this large apartment. Whether his original intention was one of reconciliation or not, I cannot say. But there, by the drawingroom fire, sat Mabel, reading with a stoicism and indifference that must have put to flight any sympathetic inclinations the Colonel may have had when he arrived. His opening remark to her is unprintable, I fear. But the remainder of his uninterrupted monologue ran somewhat like this: "You must be aware that you have not lived up to the ancient and honourable name of MacGregor. . . . And, by the way, where are those two volumes concerning my kinsman, General Sir Charles MacGregor, one of the Crown's most gallant and respected servants in India? I cannot find them anywhere. . . . You must have stolen them. . . . That you, who have traduced the honourable name, should now see fit to make off with such volumes just proves——." And so on.

All the old ladies in the drawingroom had suspended

their knitting and crocheting by this time, and were either sneaking out, or unobtrusively keeking round to witness further developments. As he could get no answer from Mabel, who remained by the fire without turning a hair, rather regarding her husband as a maniac who *might* come to his senses if completely ignored, he left the room to search the hotel for his wife's bedroom, where he hoped to discover those wretched volumes. (Incidentally, he had given them to Mabel as a marriage present!!) One of them consisted of nothing more than a wearisome compendium of genealogical tables, enabling Sir Charles, and therefore us, to trace our ancestry back to Kenneth MacAlpin, first King of Scots. The other volume, if I remember rightly, was a long-winded narrative of a journey Sir Charles had made in 1875 through the province of Khorassan, on the north-west frontier of Afghanistan.

Room by room, floor by floor, he searched for them, without let or hindrance. The hotel staff, terrified by this performance, was unable to intervene; and, since the Colonel was friendly with the entire police force, who admired his carriage and strength, there was no purpose in summoning *its* aid. It did not matter to him into which bedrooms he went, and whether he found the residents in varying degrees of unpreparedness. The situation did not admit of the polite formality of knocking before entering. Those relatively useless books had to be found before he quitted the premises.

At length, sounds of the descending Colonel echoed through the hotel. Obviously he had discovered something, for he was now grunting to himself in suppressed satisfaction. What do you think he had found? The large plaid of MacGregor tartan, spread upon our mother's bed! This was as a red rag to a bull. All thoughts of our illustrious kinsman vanished at sight of the tartan—at sight of this indignity, I should say. That a woman who, in his estimation, had shown herself so unworthy of the name of MacGregor, should still carry the glorious patronymic was bad enough, and had to be tolerated until other arrangements could be made. But, that she should add insult to injury by disporting the clan tartan on her bed, was monstrous. Something would have to be done about it, and that right early!

Picture the scene, then, when the Colonel, arrayed in Highland garb, re-entered the drawingroom with the plaid bundled under his arm! Turning to us children, who meanwhile had become transfixed with awe, he addressed us with full dramatic solemnity. " Children! " he began, " your mother has disgraced the tartan of an ancient and historic race. Never must she be allowed to disgrace it again! "

Thereupon he strode up to the fireplace and, crumpling up the plaid, threw it with theatrical effect on the enormous fire. By that fireplace he stood as one on guard, poking the plaid farther and farther into the heart of the fire with his walking-stick, until every vestige of it was consumed. Such visitors as had remained to see the fun now began to file out with smarting eyes and irritated throats. Actually, they were fumigated out.

One would have thought, of course, that Mabel had been guilty of some grave misdemeanour. But not a bit of it. Hers was the artistic temperament, wholly unsuited to a man of my father's age and eccentricities. Throughout the whole of this drama she sat, quietly reading by the fireside, as though nothing out of the ordinary were happening. Poor, darling Mabel! Her heroism was epic. But things might have gone so much better for everyone concerned, had she been born with a little less heroism in her make-up, and a little more sympathy and resilience.

* * * * *

Sweetest and most comforting of all my memories of Inverness are those associated with a very Highland family named Strachan, whom our father had known all his days, and with whom he had always spent at least part of his leave when he returned from the East, long before I was born. The Strachans are one of the few families in my life about which I am deeply sentimental. They lived in a house to which, after all these years, I could go blind-fold. That house stands in Hill Terrace, to the east of the institution for the blind; and every springtime, when I see the first of the crocuses, I remember those little clusters of yellow ones that showed themselves rather timidly in the sparse plot by their doorstep.

The Strachans hailed from remote Barvas, in Lewis, where their father, a very learned man, had been parish minister for nearly half a century. Of his learning we often had heard the Colonel tell. Was he not cited in the *New Statistical Account* as the authority for certain information it contained? And what, to our young minds, could be more authoritative than that? There was his name in print, for all the world to see! All the Strachans conversed fluently in the Gaelic. We spent more time in their house than in our own. This applied to the Colonel as well as to his children, since Annie Mary Strachan shared with him an obsession for Gaelic music, and would often sit a round of the clock with him, helping him with the arrangements of his Gaelic songs, or in tutoring vocal competitors for the annual Mòd. Annie Mary was an accomplished pianist; and her flair for Highland music was remarkable. She had a good knowledge of the theory of music too, and an accurate ear. In all this she had a considerable advantage over the Colonel who, though passionately fond of *certain* music (chiefly his own compositions!), really had no technical knowledge of it, and whose ear at times was provokingly faulty. Annie Mary and he had many a 'scene' in the Strachans' drawing-room; but in the end, after much shouting at one another, she was able to reduce to staff notation, and finally arrange for publication, many of his own Gaelic songs. The next task they undertook together was the training of potential competitors. In this field they were highly successful: many of their *protegés*, instructed in the musical side of test pieces by Annie Mary, and in the Gaelic by the Colonel, carried off prizes for three or four years in succession.

This collaboration was laudable from every point of view; but, for all Annie Mary's efforts at explaining to my father the simplest rudiments of music, and my own efforts in later years, to his dying day he was unable to appreciate the significance even of a musical interval. And he was very wild when Willie Strachan, the brother, excused his inability to understand certain musical terms by remarking that this was *a limitation often found in poets*! Though the Colonel and Willie had been friends since the latter was an infant in arms, he never quite forgave poor Willie for this well-intentioned observation. For a while it seriously curtailed their cooperation in the sphere of pipe-music. Willie was, and still is, a grand piper. He has formed any number of pipe-bands throughout Canada, where he has spent the last quarter of a century; and he is always prominent among the judges at piping contests in that Dominion.

One day recently, when looking through some old, family papers, I came upon a music manuscript containing several of the better known Gaelic melodies arranged for voice and piano by Annie Mary Strachan. This manuscript she gave me in an idle moment, a year or two before her death. It embraces her arrangements of some of my father's own compositions, set down during their long collaboration. As I held it my hands, turning it over leaf by leaf to refresh my memory, it diffused a strangeness as of something sacred, yet irretrievable. At the foot of each piece was Annie Mary's signature; and here and there were marginal corrections in the Gaelic made by my father. For me this faded document is as the mute memorial of past delights, of stilled ecstasies.

It was Annie Mary who carried me through the first intricacies of musical theory. Every Saturday forenoon she gave me a music-lesson. After I had attained some proficiency with the five-finger exercises, she started me on my first elementary tune, which, I remember, was in polka time. In order to inculcate a sense of rhythm, she sat by my side to thump out the time with her foot, and to sing into my ear, in deaving fashion, the following words that went with that first simple melody:

> My Auntie *Jean* came from *France*,
> To teach *me* the polka *dance*:
> First on the *heel*, then on the *toe*,
> That's the *way* the polkas *go*.

After an hour of Annie Mary's tuition, I felt a bit exhausted; but the customary cup of cocoa in the sitting-room thereafter was a cherished restorer. For all her impatience, she had a curious gift for teaching, and by her sheer enthusiasm evoked response in her pupils. When I made too many mistakes, she used to blast away at me in the Gaelic, just as the Colonel was in the habit of doing when anything was not quite to his liking.

Oh! the lovingkindnesses of the Strachans in our Inverness days! How could I ever forget them? Poor though they were, there was always enough to share with the Colonel and his children. Their loyalty to my father was almost tragic—so intense was it. Although they were much older than any of us children, they treated us as equals, and at the same time enveloped us in a loving care, unique in its intensity.

Poor Annie Mary was liable to spells of depression—bad bouts of Celtic Gloom—that nothing but recourse to her piano could ever banish. It was then that she used to cast aside all the sad and mournful music of the Highlands in favour of Chopin, and play herself back into sweet reasonableness. How she thrilled me with Chopin's *Polonaise in A Major*! Not since the unhappy days when Mabel played Chopin had I heard anything so painfully beautiful.

There is much more I remember about the Strachans, that family of curious genius so intimately bound up with our Inverness days. I must just mention the French musical clock that stood on their sittingroom mantelpiece, and played two melodies which I still remember. How often did the Strachans have to hide that clock's key from me!

And in my mind's eye I still see old Granny Strachan with all her faculties at the age of ninety, seated in fire-glow at evening, wrapped in her creamy shawl, stroking with long, delicate fingers a mole-coloured cat purring on her lap.

One afternoon, when wandering home from school *via* the Strachans, I witnessed an episode that never fails to recur to me when in this part of Inverness. A chimney-sweep, living on the opposite side of the street, had to get out one of his sooty ladders to rescue a black kitten that had been marooned for three days and nights on the roof of a house near by. How excited I was when the sweep descended with the wee, emaciated thing mewing in his sooty pocket! I once witnessed a somewhat similar rescue from a lofty tenement in Edinburgh, when the escape from the fire station at Lauriston had to be brought out to effect it. A large tabby had got stuck up among the chimney-pots. Spectacular as was the feat of the fireman, complete with helmet and hatchet, scooting up that interminable ladder, and descending with a cat in his arms, it had not quite the thrill about it that I felt when watching the Inverness sweep's act of quite moderate gallantry, some years previously.

* * * * *

I almost forgot to mention the Misses Middleton, three elderly sisters who lived close at hand. We marvelled at them as children, having been told that it was their father who, during the Crimean War, in his capacity as station-master at Banchory (beyond which the Deeside Railway telegraph did not extend at that time), set out over the hills on horseback for Balmoral on September 10th, 1855, to inform Queen Victoria that Sebastopol had fallen two days earlier! For this service Mr Middleton received a letter by Her Majesty's command, containing fifty pounds. This letter, "conveying her sentiments of satisfaction at his conduct on this occasion", is still preserved in the Middleton family. We children thought a great deal more of it than we did of one or two letters our own father had received from the Queen—one of them about the time of his presentation at Court, for courage and service in India and Burma. Somehow or other, they never had the flavour of anything quite so important as the fall of Sebastopol, the date of which we already had been obliged to commit to memory for examination purposes.

* * * * *

The stern physical discipline our father imposed upon us certainly contributed toward making us healthy and wiry. Years passed during which not one of us ever experienced a day's illness; but, while we were still at Inverness, Iain developed symptoms of lung trouble. It distressed us when we learnt that arrangements had been made to have him admitted to the Northern Infirmary, that he might be under proper observation and care. The effect of his leaving us was frightful, though he was going less than a mile away. Although we had had many a family bickering, we were now united in our love and prayers for little Iain. And how we sobbed that first night he did not return to the fold!

In the Infirmary he remained several weeks. On visiting days Jessie and I went faithfully to see him, bearing small gifts, and such adventure books and comic papers as we could procure. The Colonel, having been granted special facilities in virtue of his own medical qualifications, visited him twice daily. And how elated Iain was when his father presented him with a glittering five-shilling piece to celebrate his homecoming, a month or two later! Loving hands had restored him to us, cured.

CHAPTER X

FAMILY-WORSHIP

IF I WERE asked which, of all the institutions absorbing men's days, I have known the longest, unhesitatingly I would say family-worship, that admirable, Scottish custom still holding its own tolerably well in many a home north of the Tweed and Solway. More firmly fixed in my mind are my first recollections of it than is the first occasion on which I graduated at breakfast-time from saps to half an egg, though I well recall the strange experience of being allowed to decapitate my first boiled egg. Oh! the slaister I made, to use a good, Scots word!

I had been a constant attendant at family-worship at Applecross for at least a year before I realised what it was all about. Every morning and evening the Colonel assembled the household by bell, brought forth the Family Bible with meet solemnity, and read passage after passage from that ponderous and venerable tome. It naturally followed that I was well versed in the exploits of the ancient Hebrews before I could count the top row of an abacus, or had ever heard of Alice in Wonderland.

Our family was then quite small. Margaret and Catriona did not enter the world until nearly a decade later. Iain slumbered somewhere upstairs in his cot. Jessie, little more of an infant than I was, crooned away to herself, and often dropped some plaything on the floor, in this way disturbing the sanctity of our worship until it was retrieved for her, or until she was allowed to get down for it herself. Meanwhile the Colonel, heedless of her brilla-bralla, pursued his reading from the Scriptures.

One morning I heard him read: " For as Jonas was three days and three nights in the whale's belly . . ."

The woods of childhood in springtime

"As for Glen Gyle itself, father had a vague notion that he ought to have inherited . . . this ancient patrimony of the MacGregors"

Spring snows on Glen Gyle, at the head of Loch Katrine

This passage instantly arrested my attention, and induced some fresh interest in those monsters of the deep, which I used to espy from our windows as they sailed through the Sound, spouting their tall columns of vapour up toward the heavens, and frolicking and gamboling so momentously as to send quite substantial waves ashore on a calm day. No sooner was family-worship concluded than I felt impelled to rush down to our sea-gate, at the foot of the garden, to inspect the more intimately any whale that might have been passing by.

* * * * *

By the time we settled in Edinburgh, family-worship was as firmly established in the home as was breakfast. In fact, if for any reason breakfast were delayed, family-worship took precedence. We might have been obliged to do without the former: the latter we were never permitted to forego.

For years there stood at one end of the black marble mantelpiece in our father's study a pile of Bibles, six in all, four smallish ones belonging to the children (Catriona was too young to be entrusted with one as yet), and two large ones belonging to the Colonel, one in English and the other in Gaelic. The latter he used only when studying alone. The margin of almost every page of it was covered with tiny notes and annotations he had made from time to time on the innumerable occasions upon which he had read through it, from beginning to end, during his active lifetime. At the base of this pile reposed Cruden's *Concordance*, tattered through age and use.

Each week in rotation, and according to seniority, one of the four of us had to set out these Bibles in front of the family now seated round the table, and at the conclusion of worship was responsible for collecting and replacing them tidily on the mantelpiece. At the head of the table sat our father, in the rôle of president. The order of service was as follows. On Saturday and Sunday mornings at nine, when there was no school, we read aloud through the Old Testament, chapter by chapter, book by book, in strict sequence. The Colonel would announce the chapter, and then pause for a few seconds. Woe betide the dunderhead who, in failing to remember the order of the books, could not turn up his or her Bible at the correct place in a reasonable time, and might be caught having a surreptitious peep at the contents-table near the beginning! After everyone had found the place, we read aloud a chapter or two, each taking three verses in turn, and reading in accordance with the movement of the sun. This practice, incidentally, made us all aware at a very early age of the meaning of sunwise and clockwise.

When the number of verses in a particular chapter was not divisible by three, it meant that there remained a maximum of two verses. This sometimes caused disputation. Jessie would stop at the end of her three verses, deliberately leaving unread the verse or two necessary to complete the chapter. An altercation would then ensue, along the following lines:

"Just finish it, Jessie!"

"No, father. I've done my three verses. It's Alasdair's turn!"

"Do you insist on disobeying your old father?"

"Well, you see, fa——."

With a resignation that never failed to make us feel heartily ashamed of ourselves, our father read the concluding verses himself, so as to avoid further argument at prayer-time.

"Next chapter!" he then would announce by way of retribution; and the child, whose turn it was, now resumed with the first three verses, meanwhile muttering beneath his breath for Jessie to hear: "See what you've let us in for, you devil? Wait till we get you outside!"

This reading from the Old Testament was followed by a short reading from the metrical psalms and paraphrases arranged at the end of our Presbyterian Bible. Thereafter our father questioned us—*catechised* us—on what we had read. As we were expected to remember all the lengthy names of the characters and places mentioned throughout this veritable library, and he grew very wrathful when we forgot any of them, a certain degree of intelligence and vigilance was essential. Then we repaired to the big sofa, and knelt round it, with our father in the centre. After he had offered up an extempore prayer lasting four or five minutes, the Lord's Prayer had to be recited by the one whose duty it was, that particular week, to lay out and collect the Bibles. In conclusion, we all said " Amen ", in unison, and were allowed to move off to our respective pursuits at a pace regarded by the Colonel as decorous, following upon so solemn a ceremony. No rushing for the door when family-worship was over! Anyone observed making an unseemly exit was instantly summoned with an air of grand punctilio to return, that he or she might walk out slowly and with due composure. The transition from things eternal to things temporal had to be carried out with decorum.

In the evening the family again assembled for worship, and read through a couple of chapters from the *New* Testament. Sometimes, too, the Shorter Catechism was introduced on these occasions.

Finally, before clambering into bed, each of us knelt for some minutes by his or her bedside, making still further petitions to God, that He might watch over us throughout the night. Our extempore prayers at bedtime were modelled on those the Colonel offered up with such eloquence at family-worship. So much did I then believe in the literal hell of fire and brimstone that if, on the point of falling asleep, I suddenly realised I had left my personal supplications unsaid, I would get out of bed and go down on my knees in penitence.

* * * * *

If there were one aspect of family-worship I remember more clearly than another, it was Jessie's indiscipline. Wheedle her as our father might, he never was able to enlist even the semblance of attention on her part. If she were not falling into a stupor of sleep with sheer boredom, she was moving restlessly on the horse-hair seat of her chair. If she were not half asleep, or yawning very noticeably, something would be pricking her with constant irritation. It never occurred to her that the more inattentive she was, or the more she interrupted the even tenor of our worship, the longer she delayed its conclusion.

"What in the name of God is the matter, Jessie?" the Colonel would ask, when he could endure her fidgeting no longer.

Anxious to make the most of such an opening, she would get up from her chair, and begin to search the seat of it with the palm of her hand for the sharp end of a protruding horse-hair.

"Any excuse! Any excuse!" our father would exclaim in dolorous tones. "Any excuse for not hearing The Word!"

This phrase, like so many of the Colonel's, became a family aphorism.

Jessie's inattentiveness was truly shocking, though occasionally it could be very amusing. Sometimes, after she had read through her own three verses, she would quickly count twelve ahead, place her finger at the thirteenth, and then quietly dose off for a little. As her turn approached again, one of us would have to nudge her unostentatiously, or bring her back to consciousness with a little foot-work under the table. Quite often by this time her finger had moved a little, with the result that she either began at a verse that already had been read, thus giving herself away completely, or omitted one or two verses entirely. In either case, it called forth the Colonel's wrath; and he would blast away at her in the Gaelic, using intricate phrases and petitions in that language that we did not understand until we were much older.

Jessie read very quickly—so quickly, indeed, that it annoyed our father exceedingly. Words lost all their value, all their dignity, at the rate at which she galloped through them. How often was this impressed upon Jessie! But it made no difference, for she was stubborn at times. I myself read very badly. Sheer nervousness simply paralysed me. Iain, on the other hand—Iain the Paragon—read intelligently, and with perfect enunciation. Verily, he was his father's refuge in tribulation at time of prayer.

When, in the course of our reading, we arrived at the naughtier passages, or came upon some of the more indelicate words, we were bidden by the Colonel to skip them.

" Verse 16, Alasdair! " he would interject, on scenting something a little unsavoury ahead.

" But what about verses 14 and 15, father? " I would enquire meekly.

" Verse 16! " he would repeat with threatening emphasis.

This accommodation, however, did not preclude us from secretly referring to verses 14 and 15 afterwards, with the aid of *Chambers's Twentieth Century Dictionary*, that unfailing, family stand-by. Indeed, at the conclusion of family-worship this classic was often in serious demand. For priority to consult it as a means of interpreting some particularly improper passage, we occasionally came to blows.

I remember a mad rush we all made for it, arising out of our father's unsatisfactory treatment of a question put to him by one of us. Once, while reading Jeremiah, the bright idea struck him that, by way of experiment, the usual examination procedure should be reversed, so that we might question *him* regarding any doubts or difficulties we had. There were so many things about which we had wanted to ask him.

" What does the lewdness of thy whoredom mean, father? " Iain enquired.

This first question so embarrassed him that the experiment was never repeated.

* * * * *

As you may imagine, family-worship in our household had its humorous as well as its sterner moments.

" How many of the twelve Apostles can you name, Jessie? "

"Matthew, Mark, Luke, John," Jessie began at terrific speed, and with supreme confidence, "Acts, Ro—o—o—o." She clung to the o in Romans with an uncomfortable suspicion that she had started off on the wrong tack, as usual. And then she would say under her breath: " Iain, tell me just the first one or two of them; and I'll give you my Saturday penny."

Our father's slight deafness enabled us to conduct, in his presence, very quiet petitionings and promptings of this kind. There was no use Jessie's appealing to *me* for help, since I was about as backward as herself. We both took it for granted, however, that the precocious and knowing Iain *always* had the answer. What happened when Iain, in peevish mood, intentionally gave us a succession of *wrong* replies, I leave to your imagination.

Jessie habitually misquoted the Scriptures when endeavouring to emphasise some point. " All right! You can *keep* your filthy lucas! " she once told her father, when with firmness he declined her request for a penny. Lucas bells and lamps were the vogue then; and she often had heard the name in connection with such bicycle accessories.

When answering her father's catechism, she always relied implicitly on her inaccurate phonetic memory. " *Mene, Mene, tickle a parson*," she replied when asked for the writing on the wall.

" Mene, Mene *what*? " growled our father, desirous that his family should include among its learning a word or two of Hebrew.

" *Mene, Mene, tickle a parson*," she repeated with her usual self-assurance.

Family-worship or no, even the Colonel had to laugh at that!

Once, after our perusal of the third chapter of the Gospel according to St. John, he subjected us to oral examination in the approved manner.

" To whom did Jesus say ' Except a man be born again,

he cannot see the Kingdom of God?' " he now asked, turning to Jessie, in the hope that he had put to her something quite elementary in its simplicity.

"Don't tell me, father! Don't tell me!" retorted Jessie, assuming a demeanour of earnestness with which we were all familiar in such circumstances. After a moment's pause and feigned cogitation, she continued: "Eh, what's the first syllable again?"

"Nic," said the Colonel, anxious to help out where he thought there might have been a genuine lapse of memory.

"Nic—Nic—Nic," muttered Jessie, feeling intuitively for the rest of the name. "Oh, of course!" she proceeded, waving her hand with great assurance—"Nicotine!" She had heard this word once or twice in connection with our father's pipe-cleaners, and thought she might just chance it.

The roars of laughter that ensued from the remainder of us saved the situation from developing into one of dolour and grief, since the Colonel was just waiting an opportunity for indulging in one of his depressing monologues—one of his moaning lamentations—that he had been cursed with children who, with the exception of Iain, were imbeciles. Jessie's performance at family-worship often gave him cause to wonder whether she or I were the greater blockhead. Her quite meaningless ejaculations, when caught napping during Bible-reading, certainly had a spice of originality about them, of which *I* never was capable. And her cocksureness, when she well knew how fantastic were her answers, was truly remarkable. Nevertheless, she remained her father's favourite; and he countenanced in her things for which any other member of the family would have been chastised severely.

Sometimes our scriptural reading gave rise to a poser or two. These, as a rule, originated with Iain or with the Colonel himself—the two brainy ones of the family. Little was expected of Margaret or Catriona in this direction, since they were scarcely more than infants. Margaret had to attempt her three verses, however, when her turn came round.

Biblical inconsistencies disturbed our father from time to time. Always swithering in his admiration for David, for example, he frequently volunteered the observation that he found it a little difficult to understand why God should have singled out David for special honours, and allowed him to be an ancestor of Christ. The sanctification of the man who had placed Uriah in the forefront of the battle, that he might misbehave with his relict, seemed to him so irreconcilable that he simply had to dismiss the matter with the infallible comment that "we frail creatures cannot see into the mind of God, nor yet comprehend his purpose."

Biblical conundrums, of course, were never encouraged in the home. Only when the Colonel appeared in a safe humour did we dare put one to him. "Who are the two smallest men mentioned in the Bible?" we once asked him. He affected to be very shocked when we replied with Bildad the Shoe-height, and the Centurion who slept in his watch!

There was one notorious occasion on which Iain and I raised our father's ire to a white heat. One morning, as we were all solemnly clustered round the horse-hair sofa, he and I, kneeling at opposite ends of it, let go a little clockwork engine. Fairly accurate in the matter of direction, it rattled to and fro along the waxcloth border under the sofa. It made a certain amount of noise, of course. But, taking advantage of the Colonel's deafness, and by both of us coughing simultaneously whenever it was released, so as to drown any suspicion of our prank, it travelled many times, undetected, beneath that sofa during prayers. Finally, however, on the return journey from Iain's end, it went off its course, banged into our praying father's knee, and capsized just as he was on the point of reaching his peroration. Imagine our horror when he stopped suddenly, and put down his hand to discover a tiny cog-wheel of shining tin, gnawing away at his knickerbockers! There then followed what I believe to have been the most humiliating volley of denunciation we had ever brought down upon ourselves. We fled, and for the rest of the day had to be fed surreptitiously through the letter-box by one of the maids. But for Jessie's charitable intervention, we certainly would have been given a good hiding.

* * * * *

In quietly reflecting upon those years of family-worship, I often have felt since that, whatever one's religion may be, and even if one profess to having no religion at all, no one is truly enlightened who knows nothing of the Scriptures, and goes through life ignorant of their amazing bibliography. He is uneducated—uncultured, if you prefer—who is unfamiliar, for instance, with *Nunc Dimittis*, that exquisite fragment of language uttered by Simeon, who had waited so long and devoutly for the consolation of Israel:

> *Lord, now lettest thou thy servant depart in peace,*
> *according to thy word:*
> *For mine eyes have seen thy salvation,*
> *Which thou hast prepared before the face of all people——*
> *A light to lighten the Gentiles,*
> *and the glory of thy people, Israel.*

Reviewing the Bible merely as literature, there is nothing in the whole annals of mankind that even remotely vies with it. And the amount that the literature of the world has borrowed or adapted from it is colossal. Examine even our own English tongue. So numerous are the names, phrases, and figures of speech we have taken direct from these ancient Jewish writings that the mere enumeration of them would require a book to itself. The Bible, of course, is not so much a book as a library, as Jerome so aptly described it. As such it is unique. Its influence is world-wide, and is by no means so confined, as many of us imagine, to what we are pleased to term Western Civilization. Thanks largely to the Colonel's ideas of bringing up a family, the Bible is the only piece of literature that astounds me absolutely.

As a family, we must have read through the Testaments round the table, from Genesis to Revelation, at least a dozen times, under our father's supervision and guidance. And I in no way exaggerate when I say that, to this training and discipline in the Scriptures, I ascribe such facility as I may have with the English language.

I am told that nowadays a devout knowledge of Holy Writ is unusual among children. But during my childhood in Scotland, thirty years ago or thereby, the Bible was nothing more or less than God's Word, set down, in English, by God Himself. Any tampering with it, any revising of it—in short, anything but the plain Authorised Version—was sacrilege, punishable by eternal damnation. We were taught to regard any questioning of its authority as particularly heinous. We believed implicitly that the world had been created in six days of twenty-four hours each; that the Ark came to rest on Ararat; that the sun had stood still upon Gibeon, and the moon in the valley of Ajalon; and that Jonah had spent three days and three nights in the belly of the whale. And I doubt whether we were any the worse for our literal belief.

As for the Bible, a true church, shorn of senseless ritual, but founded upon the wisdom and inspiration of that colossal document, is the only channel, it appears to me, through which man the barbarian may become man redeemed.

CHAPTER XI

THE SABBATH

THE OTHER day I received from Calgary a letter written by a Highlander who had known us intimately many, many years ago, and who, on hearing that I contemplated this book, set out for me all the things he could remember about us in the hope that some of them might be of value to me. That letter contained one sentence relating to my father that struck me forcibly. " Rather strange for one with his Radical tendencies, and one who had travelled so extensively, and had encountered so many religious sects, that all his life he was a firm believer in Christ and all the Bible says."

I hardly think the Colonel took the Bible just as literally as my correspondent's words might suggest. Yet, I do know how true an estimate of the man is contained in that sentence. And I like to ponder it sometimes, now that he has passed beyond my immediate ken.

Despite this belief in Christ, however, or perhaps because of it, he never could bring himself to partake of the Sacrament. We attended church with him on Communion Sundays, just as on ordinary Sundays. The only difference was that we did not occupy our usual pew, but sat in that part of the church set aside for the very few who were not communicants. On the way home from church we sometimes ventured to enquire of him why he did not join in the Communion Service with the rest of the grown-ups. To our questioning—to our inquisitiveness—we never obtained a reply. We always had the feeling that this was one of the very personal and sacred matters on which we were not entitled to enlightenment. For a while we had a suspicion that, for some reason or other, he was debarred. In our history books we had read of the Wolf of Badenoch, who had been *excommunicated*; and it occurred to us that, maybe, our gallant father had committed some serious misdemeanour with similar result. As we grew older, however, we realised that a Presbyterian was not excommunicable; and so we were still without an explanation.

Of our first church in the Highlands I need not say much. I already have written of it in *The Goat-Wife*. Suffice it to say that it was United Free, and that we were obliged to attend it with the strictest regularity. I doubt whether even toothache was a sufficient pretext for absence. Woe betide the member of the family who, in the Colonel's view, was malingering when the church bells called! On Sunday afternoons we attended Sunday-school with the same punctilio.

When removing from one locality to another, the Colonel was careful to see that, as in the case of our secular education, there should be no break in church attendance. The rigid insistence with which Victorian and Edwardian parents dragged their begotten to church, where they so often sat in boredom, largely explains their disinclination to identify themselves with this institution in later life.

We had been in Inverness but a day or two when Sunday found us all in the Strachans' pew at the West Parish Church—in the front seat of the gallery, facing the pulpit. We were a little astonished at this adherence, since this was the Established, or Auld, Kirk, and we had been reared on the principles of the United Free. The minister of the West Parish in those days was the Rev. Gavin Lang, father of Matheson Lang, brother of the Rev. Marshall Lang, and therefore uncle of the Archbishop of Canterbury. Old Gavin Lang impressed us greatly as children. We hardly understood his dialectics, of course; but we did admire his height and his grand countenance. His grey beard was the trimmest we had ever seen. We thought it a better one even than King Edward's, coloured reproductions of whom we so often had seen on enamel mugs at

Sunday-school soirees, and on china ornaments in Highland homes. Mr Lang must have been at least six foot four, which brings to mind the occasion when a friend of mine remarked to one of his parishioners, some years after his retirement: "I'm sorry to see your old minister has so much difficulty in getting about."

"Ay, it's that end of him that's gone first," was the parishioner's succinct reply, as the agèd minister shochled past them.

We and the Lang family saw quite a lot of one another in those days. Probably this explains how I am more interested in Matheson Lang than in most actors. Occasionally, he was to have been seen in the manse pew, along with his brother, Jim. I say 'occasionally' because by this time he had left Inverness to all intents and purposes, and only returned on holiday from time to time. Poor Jim fell in the Great War.

Matheson was then a youth of about eighteen, in no way as striking in appearance as his brother, who was two years older. A visit of Frank Benson's company to Inverness had settled his career. That incident in the manse diningroom, about which he himself writes so amusingly,* had already taken place—the staging of the fight from *Romeo and Juliet*. Pandemonium reigned; and Mr Lang, consumed with fury, strode out of the study to investigate his sons' behaviour.

"What's the meaning of this appalling uproar?"

"It means that I'm going to be an actor," Matheson replied.

Horror! There was a deadly silence. That moment was the turning-point in Matheson's life.

By the time I first saw Matheson on the stage, he had become quite illustrious. I managed to get a seat in the front row of the orchestra stalls. And how I longed to say to him: "Oh! Matheson! Do give some indication that you remember me! Don't you recall those Sundays at the West Parish Church, and the two little brothers in

* *Mr. Wu Looks Back* (Stanley Paul, 1941).

red kilts who used to walk home along the river with you and Jim afterwards? And how we prayed that your father's sermon might not be too long?"

* * * * *

The kirk-goers of the North were so sure of themselves and their doctrines. The more pious of them were content to explain the God of Love in terms of everlasting damnation, and of the cruellest passages in the Old Testament. Even then, there seemed to me to be something strangely incongruous about many of their beliefs, something unreal and often insincere in the ease and confidence with which passages could be interpreted to justify this, or condemn that, according to the requirements of the particular believer.

Certain biblical conceptions were utterly repulsive to me. Reference to being washed in the Blood of the Lamb conjured up in my mind the picture of a ghastly bath. Religion should never be presented in such terms, since it suggests more of pagan slaughter and sacrifice than of the Christ as I have liked to understand Him.

By the same token, one might say something about that frightful and frightening sense of sin which our Victorian and Edwardian parents implanted in us. Strange, is it not, that, whereas parents of that generation would have gone to any length to protect their children from physical pain or illness, yet they revelled in creating in their undeveloped minds a sense of sin and shame that might easily have upset their reasoning faculties?—and, indeed, quite often did, as we now know?

To most ministers and elders of Scotland thirty or forty years ago, the idea of child innocence was as repugnant as the view that there was no eternal hell-fire. As children brought up in the Highlands, we were made to understand that from birth, irrespective of our efforts for personal betterment here on earth, the likelihood of our being caught up in some everlasting conflagration was better than that of avoiding such a fate. It appeared as though all of us were doomed to a fair spell of the pains and writhings of hell. The only consolation permitted us was that, while all persons having heard of Jesus Christ were earmarked for the flames if they failed to be one hundred per cent. righteous, Jesus, in His mercy, *might* intercede with God to stretch a point, as it were, when dealing with the nigger children of Africa, who may never have heard of Him and His Salvation. We were taught to believe that the nigger children were condemned to something not quite so terrible as the hell of fire and brimstone awaiting *us*. But care was always taken to make it palpably plain that they were *condemned*, and that their condemnation, like our own, was forever and evermore.

Hell was the punishment meted out to us by God for our general sins on week-days, and for our particular waywardnesses on the Sabbath. So much that was perfectly fitting during the week was anathema on Sundays. Our Presbyterian upbringing in the Highlands, and even to some extent in Edinburgh at a later date, emphasised this distinction. By a rigid interpretation of the Fourth Commandment, on Sundays certain things were forbidden that even many reputable ministers of the Gospel now do on that day with the clearest conscience. Music in our home on the Seventh Day, for example, was something the Colonel would not tolerate. The mere idea of touching the piano on the Sabbath provoked his frowns: if the idea developed into practice, it produced a brain-storm.

Now and again Mabel risked a few notes; but she had to be careful to confine her efforts to *The Holy City* and similar compositions. Even these the Colonel disapproved. Imagine, then, the effect it had upon us children when, on coming to Inverness, we found the Salvation Army playing trumpets and cornets in the streets on Sunday mornings, and to the glory of God! This upset all our religious calculations, and that conception of the Sabbath upon which we had been reared so diligently. A quarter of a century later, when the Colonel was an octogenarian, and had lost his reading sight, he frequently spent a drowsy Sunday afternoon, listening to secular music on the wireless. Not that he ever *enjoyed* it, especially if it happened to be a pianoforte recital, since he regarded the piano at any time as an effeminate instrument, and in no way to be compared with the bagpipes!

For several years the most we were permitted to do on the Sabbath, apart from family-worship, church, and Sunday-school, was to go for a quiet, dignified walk in the afternoon. It was certain damnation to enter a shop, even to purchase a ha'penny copy of the Shorter Catechism, let alone sweetmeats. By some curious dispensation, it was possible to procure a ha'penny slab of treacle toffee and a ha'penny Catechism in the same shop. In the windows of such sweetie-shops as were open in Edinburgh on Sundays, one might see the Shorter Catechism exposed for sale among india-rubbers and pencils, liquorice and sherbet-dabs.

Lesson-books were strictly prohibited. Only secular publications with a strong religious bias, such as *The Pilgrim's Progress* or *The Peep of Day*, were allowed to remain even in sight on the Sabbath. If we had not mastered our homework by Saturday evening, we would have to bear the consequences at school the following Monday. Nevertheless, we occasionally did a little homework on Sundays, but surreptitiously. It was usually done behind some bulky piece of furniture. The drawingroom sofa was an admirable screen: so, too, was the door of the drawing-room cupboard. Kneeling at a small chair placed behind that door Iain would snatch a few moments with his precious stamp-album on the rare occasions when father had forgotten to lock it away. Unlike Jessie and me, Iain never used this hidie-hole for homework on Sundays; but on week-days he might be found there, holding a penny bottle of ink in his left hand and a pen in his right, dashing off his ' ekkies ' a few minutes before hurrying off to school. In a manner that, to me, seemed very remarkable, he usually obtained full marks, and most of the prizes that were going at the close of the session. A month with pen and ink behind that cupboard door would never have

"... *our father never allowed us to forget the land of our MacGregor forbears*"

Loch Lomond at Inversnaid

" Swear by the Grey Stane on Inch Cailleach ! "

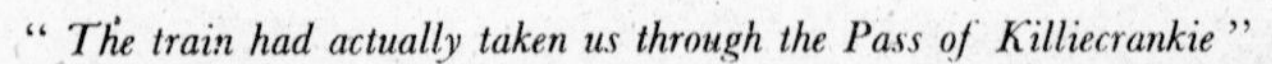

" The train had actually taken us through the Pass of Killiecrankie "

brought me anything more than the bang on the side of the head, with which my school-day usually opened.

The discipline of those Sabbatarian times was both terrific and morbid. One seldom had the courage to enter a Presbyterian church the fraction of a second after the service had begun; and certainly no one ever had the temerity to leave until the Benediction had been pronounced, however lengthy and tedious the preacher's discourse. Such irregularities would attract the disapproving eye of every devout worshipper. This was not a matter merely of self-consciousness: it was cold fact and usage. The comparative ease and informality of Roman Catholic and Anglican Churches would have seemed very irreverent to us in those days. If you felt a little restless in church—if something actual or fancied were kittling you—if thick woollens were irritating your skin to the point of excruciation—you had to thole it in true Calvinistic style. I do not think for a moment that John Calvin exacted this sort of martyrdom; but this was largely how his teaching was then interpreted in Presbyterian Scotland. Oh! those woollies! I never knew which I hated the more—them, or the kirk!

As for work on the Sabbath, we were prohibited from doing this and from doing that, which meant that we were prevented from doing anything the least pleasurable. This literal enforcement of the Fourth Commandment was all very well; but it was never quite explained to us why our maids had to labour and do all their menial work on the Sabbath, very much as on week-days. They were obliged to make beds, and prepare the traditional Scottish Sunday dinner for one o'clock, in defiance—so it appeared to me, at any rate—of the law of Moses. All the work which, on the Sabbath, we continued to regard as *absolutely necessary*, seemed to be precisely the work among man-servants and maidservants that the Fourth Commandment was designed to abolish.

CHAPTER XII

DISCIPLINE IN THE HOME

THE COLONEL was certainly a disciplinarian. Yet, I am not slow to admit that the element of regimentation in the home, and the restraint it inculcated, have stood me in better stead than has all the book learning with which he tried to endue me. The regularity of family-worship, for instance, and the code of conduct bound up with it, were an excellent training. They did much to teach one self-control.

A sense of discipline pervaded every action throughout the entire day, which began whenever the Colonel thought everyone should be up and about. Of few things in life was he more intolerant than of the morning sluggard. Sleepiness at rising-time called forth raucous commands from him, which shook every bed in the house. This may have been attributable to some extent to his own insomnia. Like so many who do not sleep too well, he could not thole the idea of anyone else slumbering a moment longer than he thought necessary. Both Iain and I shared a distaste for early rising, and a corresponding predilection for going to bed as late as possible. " Always lively at the wrong end of the day ! " father would complain, when we became particularly wakeful and communicative at midnight. This trait of bedding late, and of sleeping long the following morning, is very Highland, probably very Celtic. The Highlanders certainly have never been famed for their early rising, never been noted for their ability to catch the early worm. In support of my own personal sloth, I once had the temerity to quote from Stephen Leacock's *Literary Lapses*: " The time to get up is when you *have* to, and not before."

"Don't quote any damned American to me!" thundered the Colonel. "The time to get up is when I say so!"

The real discipline of the home began the moment the Colonel roused its sleepy-headed inmates. Any sign of yawning thereafter he greeted with such derision that it had to be performed noiselessly, and in secret, with the palm of the hand covering as much as possible of the accompanying grimace.

By way of fortifying us against the bodily ills afflicting so much of mankind, he always insisted that oatmeal should remain a staple article in our dietary. Thus we had porridge for breakfast every morning of our lives, except on Sundays, when it was held that the preparation of the same might prevent the maids from getting to kirk in the forenoon. Eggs in one form or another were substituted on that morning. With regard to the porridge, the Colonel, despite all his travels, never lost the notion that this was a manly dish, and could be enjoyed only when it answered to the traditional Scottish recipe, as handed down from the time of Bannockburn. The sprinkling of sugar over it he viewed with contempt. The fellow who could not take his porridge, unadulterated, was a craven, unworthy of his ancestors. Sugar reduced this national and historic dish—this dish so loved of the Celtic kings and heroes since Fingalian times—to something effeminate and sybaritic. A little treacle or cloying golden syrup, however, was excusable now and then, but never sugar. Why this distinction, we never understood.

Moreover, father insisted that the family should be nourished as much as possible on such wholesome faring as oatcakes, herrings, and Scotch broth. For herrings the entire household had a partiality. When one of our cousins took to sending us a firkin of salt herrings from the Hebrides at regular intervals, there was often a dispute as to whether this member of the family, or that, had had more than his due share.

The eating of sweetmeats or morsels between meals he furiously discountenanced. Regularity and abstemiousness were his motto in this connection. It infuriated him to discover any member of the household eating anything immediately before a meal, or even sucking a sweet. Nothing destroyed a healthy, normal appetite, he used to urge, like indiscriminate munching between meals. I do not think that in an intimate association with the Colonel, extending over thirty years, I ever saw him eat or drink anything, except at meal-times, apart from the one large cup of tea he sipped with religious precision at 4 p.m. To his regularity in these matters he attributed his health and longevity.

* * * * *

Our general conduct was regulated by a code as immutable, as irrefragible, as those Laws of the Medes and Persians, to which Aunt Dorothy used to allude in her more disciplinary moments. Upon *himself*, as well as upon his offspring, the Colonel imposed the strictest restraint—except in the matter of language! For instance, he was punctilious about the time he wound his watch. This he did but once in twenty-four hours, and then just as he placed it under his pillow at bed-time. Toying with the winding arrangement of a watch irritated him at any time: such fidgeting betrayed a pusillanimity of which he was intolerant.

The dog-earing of the leaves of a book was prohibited, as was the habit of wetting one's finger when turning over a page. If the careless handling of a volume resulted in the accidental displacement of his book-mark, there was never a moment's peace until the offender had been identified and duly castigated. Writing was so much more than a hobby with him that the misuse or destruction of the various materials required was deemed an unpardonable sin. Only by such a rigid attitude was he able to prevent his offspring from defacing his blotting-pad, carelessly smearing his eraser with inky fingers, playing darts with his pens, or from damaging the typewritter that provided him with so much pleasure and recreation. Bending back the covers of books, or crouching with them over the fire, annoyed him. Crouching at any time he looked upon as slovenly; but, when indulged in over the fire with a book in one's hand, it was execrable.

As for the care with which he placed things, so that he might know precisely where they were to be found, he was almost fanatical. Strictly forbidden was such deranging of his book-shelves as made it impossible for him to pick out, by rule of thumb, certain books of reference in constant use, as well as manuscripts of his own, upon which he might be working at that time. And he often waxed wrathful when, despite all his warnings and petitions, someone had removed his pipe-cleaners from that corner of the mantelpiece where nothing else was ever allowed to rest. Those were the days when one required a button-hook for boots and shoes and gaiters. Since our father wore gaiters with his knickerbockers and Norfolk jacket, heaven help brother or sister who removed from its wonted place the horn button-hook that had accompanied him round and round the world, and had never been mislaid until he married poor Mabel, and had a family! If removed when dusting, or carelessly placed at the opposite end of the mantelshelf, his curses rent the air.

Then there were rules to ensure our personal safety, as also that of the king's lieges. We were forbidden to point an air-gun or toy pistol at anyone, whether loaded or not. I once received a good spanking for having held up one of the maids with a toy pistol, and followed up this warfare with a homemade catapult. The excuse that neither catapult nor pistol was loaded made no difference. The Colonel had seen so many serious and even fatal accidents, owing to carelessness and undue familiarity with firearms and the like, that he denounced pointing in every form. Even the finger of scorn, if resorted to at all, had to be pointed but figuratively.

* * * * *

Our Spartan upbringing did much to make us hardy. Incidentally, what we children had not actually culled about the human body from our father's conversation and advice, we gained from constant reference to his threadbare copy of the *Materia Medica*.

At unexpected intervals we were assembled in order of seniority to have our teeth examined. And woe betide the one whose tooth-brush had been found in the bathroom rack, so dry as to indicate that it had not been in recent use.

Once a fortnight or thereabouts, we were arraigned for foot-and-hand inspection, lest we neglected our ablutionary obligations to them. The feet had to be maintained in a permanent state of perfection. I often have had reason to bless my father in subsequent years for his disciplinary influence in these respects. On turning to the diary I kept during the War, I am reminded of a singular instance on which it saved me from being blown to smithereens. We had arrived at an encampment of bell tents on the outskirts of Poperinghe, after a gruelling march under shell-fire and in broiling sunshine, on our way to take up fresh positions in the line at Ypres. We were all dog-tired. Two other fellows and I happened to select the tent situated at the farthest extremity of Toronto Camp. Here we were to be permitted a few hours' respite, before moving up into the trenches after dark. Close at hand ran a muddy stream; and I, with my love of water in any form whatsoever, decided to sit by its shell-holed bank for a minute or two, bathing my feet. I took off my foot-gear; and, on leaving the tent, tried to persuade the others to follow my example. They, however, were too exhausted. Down they flopped on the earth floor of the tent, too tired even to throw off their equipment. Scarcely were my feet in the muddy stream, thirty yards away, when the Germans sent over a salvo of shells in rapid succession. One of these fell so precisely on the tent as to leave nothing but a yawning crater where it had stood. All I could see, as concussion and tons of hurtling earth carried me bodily into the stream, was a mass of shattered limbs and equipment, flying in all directions. There was a roll-call shortly afterwards. No one else in the whole wide world knew whom that tent had contained; and I never would have been alive to tell the tale, but for my father's rigorous training.

* * * * *

In matters concerning the carriage and personal appearance of his children, the Colonel was most particular. "Hold yourself up like a soldier's son!" he suddenly would shout in commanding—nay, terrifying—tones, if I happened to be stooping a little when out walking with him. "Take your hands out of your pockets, and swing your arms!" In later years these outbursts used to alarm the passers-by on Edinburgh's Princes Street as much as they embarrassed me. "Poor laddie!" a sympathetic passer-by once remarked, on hearing these familiar words of command. "Colonel MacGregor's in one of his furies!"

Self-control in the use of hands and face was as much insisted upon as was deportment. "Don't be demonstrative! Don't be theatrical!" he would say, if I used my hands too much when explaining something. "Keep your hands under control! You're not a Frenchman! You're not an actor!" Gesticulation, as a substitute for the spoken word, whether by facial contortion or by gesture with the limbs, he regarded as the refuge of the inarticulate.

Few things annoyed him more than to catch one of his children in the act of pulling faces or grimacing. Even in playful mimicry this kind of thing was discountenanced. I once attempted to portray Queen Victoria as we knew her through the somewhat bloated likenesses one saw in almost every house during the first decade of the present century. By spreading a napkin over my head, I had hoped to reproduce the effect of the widow's cap. And I was in process of improving my physiognomic contortions by studying variations of them in the mirror, before inflicting them on the household, when, in the mirror also, I caught the baleful eye of my father, as he stalked up behind me, intent on giving me a clout.

* * * * *

Slovenliness in diction, slipshod enunciation, made our father very impatient. In the choice of vocabulary, too, he was particular. Certain words such as sweat and sweating were forbidden. Only navvies and lumbermen were capable of this perfectly natural function: *we* had to speak of perspiration. Only in connection with such figurative phrases as 'the sweat of one's brow' might the word be used at all. The upper classes never sweated: they always perspired. By the same token, the words, *belly-ful* and *belly-ache*, though constantly in use throughout rural Scotland, had to be avoided in our household. Guts could never be referred to. Only butchered animals, dangling from hooks in shops, had guts. Human beings, because of their spiritual superiority, possessed nothing so vulgar, nothing so indecent. They were endowed, on the contrary, with the much more refined apparatus known as intestines. If we talked of spewing, instead of vomiting, we were severely reprimanded. The pretext that the former word had recurred during our biblical readings gained no favour. The prophets of the Old Testament might have been justified in using it, but never the Colonel's bairns!

* * * * *

Our father strove to inculcate in us an interest in our personal appearance; and I remember well how an attempt to emulate him in this respect culminated in Iain's discovery of a cheap hairdresser somewhere in the Fountainbridge of Edinburgh. Here he purchased for twopence a bottle containing about a pint of crude hair-oil; and for weeks the house reeked of this balm. One could trace Iain's whereabouts entirely by nose. If he were in hiding, buried somewhere in *Comic Cuts*, refusing to answer when called, he could be tracked down quite easily by this sickening odour. He selfishly guarded his pint bottle; and I often had to bribe him with treasures that were not my own, in the hope of getting from him a teenie-weenie drop of the sacred oil.

* * * * *

While father was always ready to satisfy legitimate curiosity, there were certain subjects he would not discuss. Among these was freemasonry, which none of us was entitled to probe. Iain once enquired in confidential mood what it all signified, and, in so doing, brought such a wave of damnation upon his head that he never dared breathe a word on the subject thereafter. One Sunday, when we had pleaded successfully that it was too wet for our usual trail to church, we clandestinely turned our father's uniforms out of various trunks and drawers, and came upon all sorts of curious vestments and medals. These, we suspected, had something to do with father's secret society. He was very angry indeed when he discovered that we had not put this glittering regalia back as neatly as when we found it.

About this time there came to Edinburgh the play entitled *Are you a Mason?* The reception the Colonel gave to the suggestion that some of us might be allowed to go to see it only intensified our belief that masonry was, indeed, a mysterious cult. Gradually, however, we began to look upon it as so much hush and humbug. Of course, even such masons as have been shown up to satiety, as Stevenson wrote, preserve a kind of pride; " and not a grocer among them, however honest, harmless, and empty-headed he may feel himself to be at bottom, but comes home from one of their coenacula with a portentous significance of himself."

I once quoted this passage to father on his return from a masonic function. I need hardly describe the reception given to it by a man whose constant boast it was that at one time he had been Director of Ceremonies of Freemasonry in India!

Apropos my father's strict code, I once had the imprudence to remark that stealing, after all, could not be so heinous an offence. Had we not been nurtured very largely on the deeds of our ancestor, Rob Roy?—encouraged to dwell on his achievements as a black-mailer and a cattle-riever? " That's a very different matter!"

roared the Colonel. "*He* stole to give to the poor: *you* stole for yourself!" He had in mind two incidents which occurred about this time, when I was eight or nine years old.

I had developed the habit of paying occasional visits to my mother's tartan hand-bag, which hung all too conveniently on a bell-handle by the fire-side. I sometimes sneaked into the sittingroom to help myself to a shilling from it, before dashing off to school. As she herself admitted when, ultimately, I confessed my guilt, she was aware of these peculations: yet, she allowed me to rob her of several shillings before calling me to account.

One morning, however, I overstepped the limit of prudence—I abstracted a florin! The possession of so large a coin gave me considerable anxiety. As I could not make immediate use of it, I remembered the example of Achan, of whom we had heard during family-worship, and buried my treasure at the foot of an oak, with a view to exhuming it later. Conscious of my guilt, it took considerable courage to present so large a coin at any counter in our small village; but once this difficulty was surmounted subsequent transactions gave me less anxiety.

Nevertheless, that florin was my undoing. Mabel felt that there was now no saying how far I might be tempted to go: sovereigns and half-sovereigns might be the next to disappear! And so I was called to account, and never stole from dear Mabel again.

But my reputation had suffered. Soon after this I was sent by Mabel to the neighbouring farm of Invercharron to bring back a letter bearing upon a forthcoming bazaar. On reaching the farm, Mrs Robertson, the farmer's wife, invited me to stay and play with her step-son. I required little persuasion, since the farm, with its cows and horses, its guinea-fowls and peacocks and bubbly-jocks (never to speak of the delectable tea!), was my idea of Paradise.

Toward nightfall I set out for home, bearing in my hand a letter containing coins, doubtless representing some purchase connected with the bazaar aforementioned.

When hurrying along the short-cut by the railway embankment, I stumbled. The envelope burst; and the contents shot into the long grass fringing the path. Though I searched frantically, I could not find a single coin.

"Jack, the boy's an incurable thief!" Mabel exclaimed, when I sought to explain what had happened.

I protested my innocence without avail. My explanation that it was dark when the mishap occurred went for nothing. I had failed to return with the sum of five shillings. At daybreak next morning I ran off to the embankment to search once more, but in vain. No one believed I was innocent but Mrs Robertson. It was her intervention alone that saved me from a sound thrashing.

Some years later, when holidaying with the Goat-wife at Cnocnamoine, I was walking along this very embankment when I suddenly became aware that I had arrived at the spot where, as a child, I had lost that wretched bazaar-money. I halted for a moment to look among the grass, moving it carelessly aside with my foot. I saw something small and round protruding from the earth, and, stooping, picked up a black and corroded half-crown—doubtless, one of the coins I had lost on that fateful evening.

* * * * *

Though the Colonel by no means lacked a sense of humour, and often enjoyed the simplest joke, he had a tendency to discourage laughter in the home. Only occasionally did he permit himself the relaxation suggested in the adage—

A little nonsense now and then
Is relished by the wisest men.

But he never allowed himself to be flippant for long. All his gaiety, he used to maintain, vanished the day he married my beautiful mother. Thus, he was inclined to be impatient with anyone who felt humoursome when he did not. He held the view that laughter, except in homoeopathic doses, tended to deteriorate into ribaldry and vulgarity. He regarded it as cheapening and undignified, and perhaps as a little disrespectful in his presence. In matters of this kind he betrayed a peculiar streak of vanity. Banter and badinage he hated, as also the type of familiarity they engendered: they always led to a decline in mutual respect, and to quarrels in the end. When told a story, he would laugh in a vague way, rather giving the impression that any undue exhibition of mirth on his part might detract from the conception of balance and self-control which he strove to convey. Jokes about Highlanders, however, usually found acceptance with him, especially those illustrating the difficulties experienced by native Gaelic speakers, when first obliged to use English—a language that to them is really a foreign tongue. There was the story of Donald MacSporran, from the Gaelic-speaking Isle of Skye. Donald enlisted, and had to fill in some official papers. When he came to the question regarding any previous employment he had had, he answered it as follows: "First of aall, she wass a herring-fish [fisherman]. Then she was a broken stone [stone-breaker] at the side of the road. And then she wass a policeman and a half for a year in Glasgow."

Then there was the native of the Outer Hebrides, who had been on his first visit to the mainland. When returning by Oban, he had a few hours to put in before the steamer set out across the Minch in the early morning. These hours he spent in solitude in the gas-lit lounge of a local hotel. About 3 a.m., when on the point of leaving for the quay in the dark, he was seized with the desire to remove from the lounge something in the nature of a souvenir. What better than a gas luminant, then? It certainly would give a more powerful light than the oil lamps to which he had been accustomed all his life. So, at the last moment, he wrenched off one of the gas-brackets affixed to the walls, dropped it into his bag, and made for the steamer. On reaching his native township, he fixed the bracket to the wall of his cottage, and then assembled his neighbours to witness this braw thing he had brought home with him. He proceeded to demonstrate. Match after match he wasted, in vain endeavour, his neighbours by this time weary of watching his futile efforts. " Ah, well! " he exclaimed at last, " believe me or believe me not, she would be making a dampt good light in the Oban whateffer! "

* * * * *

Never was there so much laughter in our home as during the sojourn of Bella, an Inverness maid. We thought the world of Bella. She was the most comical person we had ever met. We lured her away from the services of a neighbour—a pure case of coveting our neighbour's maid-servant!

Bella usually made an excursion to the ' pierriotts ' on her afternoons off. Her banter the following morning was always interlarded with their songs, jokes, and patter. Her repertoire of cliché (most of it meaningless, much of it a little vulgar) was immense, and poured forth from her whether it fitted the occasion or not.

Though small and squat, with contours as chubby as a cherub's, Bella was exceedingly strong. When she rolled up her sleeves in a threatening manner, as if she meant to skelp us, we fled in all directions. She was adept at what she used to term the ' Jew Gypsy ', having been taught some painful grips by a sailor-lad who once ' coorted ' her.

Bella was prone to hysterics of laughter—tornadoes of mirth, as the film world would say. One was obliged to keep away from her when these mirthful bouts seized her, since the mere presence of a human being set her off again. Suddenly overcome with a laughing attack at the breakfast-table one morning, she dropped an ashet of greasy kippers on the Colonel's knickerbockers. For this she instantly was given notice. When, a little later, in a brave endeavour to pull herself together and behave with some sense of her position, she entered the study, armed with benzine to remove the stain, great mirth-tears were still streaming down her cheeks. The Colonel caught sight of this; and Bella, unable to resist another good laugh, broke out afresh, and so infected the Colonel that he, too, had to laugh, and felt obliged to withdraw his notice.

There were two particular phrases Bella had picked up, which she reiterated, in season and out of it. One was " My word! if I catch you bending! " You had but to stoop to pick something up in her sight to evoke this epigram. If anxious to impress one with the absolute truthfulness of some statement, when all evidence seemed to the contrary, she used to add " As sure as death! " and " As sure as gun's iron! " and " May God strike me dead! " These expressions she rattled off in quick succession. If this familiar catalogue of assurances appeared to be meeting with indifferent acceptance, she would extend her right arm above her head, and say " Hand up to God! " and conclude by drawing her right index finger firmly across her throat, saying simultaneously, and with great intensity, " Cut ma throat! "

Once, when we were all playing hide-and-seek about the house in the dark, the Colonel crept out of his study to discover what all the din was about. Bella was the seeker at the time. Noticing a figure moving stealthily near her, she stepped forth and embraced it, meanwhile giving vent to another of her favourite phrases: " Come into ma airms, ye bunch o' finnan-haddies, ma cock-eyed pet! "

It took her a week or more to recover from the attack of giggling occasioned by her discovery that she was holding the Colonel in her arms!

CHAPTER XIII

COUNTRY WAYS

THERE WERE many things I missed when I went to school at Edinburgh. I missed the glorious blaze of whin in bloom, for instance, with its nutty fragrance as of almond, even more intoxicating than the perfume of Mabel's sweetpeas and roses. And I missed the days of heather-burning and of whin-burning, though in a modified way one might have got the latter among the Pentlands or the Lammermuirs, had one travelled as far beyond the city.

The selecting of the right day for whin-burning, as country folk well know, is a ticklish affair. Really suitable conditions occur but seldom. Either the ground and undergrowth are damp, and the upper branches bone-dry, or the branches are wet with dew when the under parts are as inflammable as tinder. Or there may be too much or too little wind. Too little results in slow, ineffectual burning, often necessitating a good deal of rekindling: too much, on the other hand, carries the flames through the bushes so fiercely and quickly that they tend to get out of control. Best of all for the purpose is a fresh breeze, when there is no dampness in the atmosphere. Then it is possible to burn to the best advantage by allowing the fire to creep *against* the wind.

To all who enjoy the primitive act of lighting a fire in the open, the burning of gorse, of heather, or of bracken is one of almost furious delight. Just picture it! The flames shooting and roaring heavenward; the sizzling and crackling, the hissing and spluttering, of moist reeds and rushes and pine-needles within reach of the ring of fire, ever extending as it advances; the vibrating warmth;

the clouds of hot smoke, carrying with them across the landscape a redolence strange and primitive; the agility with which a flame attacks an isolated tussock, reducing it to a black, smouldering protuberance; the innermost flames underneath the burning bush, glowing like incandescent gas mantles with the slightest whiff of wind; the satisfaction derived from starting such a conflagration with a box of matches, a bit of dry paper, and perhaps a drop of paraffin-oil carried in a wee bottle for the purpose; the excitement of skipping from bush to bush, bearing a torch of hissing needles, conveying the fire from one to another; the white ashes lying so still and warm when the fury of the blaze is spent; the charred ghosts of shrubs and young trees through which, alas! such fire has passed.

This burning often leaves a weird and unsightly spectacle, scarring the prospect for several months, until the young, green shoots begin to re-appear with added vigour, freed from choking weeds or accumulations of old and decaying vegetable matter. It has been estimated that hill pasture, properly treated by fire, yields sustenance for bestial at least three weeks earlier than otherwise.

I have not had a day's whin-burning since those memorable times with Aunt Dorothy at Cnocnamoine, except on the occasion when I spent a few days' leave at Upperwood, a farm on the Black Isle, situated on the hillside behind Jemimaville, overlooking the Cromarty Firth. That was in 1918. I had come back to enjoy the ploy in which a son of the home would have shared, had he not fallen at Arras in the spring of the previous year. That whin-burning on the moor impinging upon this farm had a touch of sadness and unreality about it.

Though circumstances seem to have precluded me in recent years from the actual burning, I have revelled a good deal in whin-lands enflamed in blossom. Shall I ever forget, for instance, the whins at Dallachy, in Moray—that vast expanse of golden bloom between Port Gordon and Spey Bay—or the whin-moor between Fort George and Ardersier? The whin bloom on the farther side of

"On reaching that stretch of the Garry near Blair-Atholl, one begins to realise that the Highlands lie behind, and the Lowlands ahead"

"In time of severity, the traveller in these parts may even come upon a herd of deer lying upon the snow, dead from starvation"

Where the mountain-road to Applecross traverses the Pass of the Cattle

the Blackford Hill, at Edinburgh, or at the Duddingston end of the King's Park, high up among the crags culminating in Arthur's Seat, was a poor show in comparison with what might be seen in season at Dallachy or at Fort George, though even this had its compensations for one who had been accustomed in early years to wandering so freely among the whinny tracts of the North.

A country upbringing certainly eases one's passage through life. It enables one to enjoy the winter as well as the summer. It inculates a personal indifference to weather, making it possible to feel at home in the open, whether in sunshine or in rain. It gives one a familiarity with the beasts of the field, and removes the fear that town-bred folks often have of horses and cows, and even of poultry. (Geese and turkey-cocks can be very obstreperous at times, you know!) It produces confidence and a sureness of foot in wet or slippery conditions. It trains the senses of sight and of hearing to a remarkable degree. It increases one's powers of adaptability, and helps one to find all sorts of uses for all sorts of things. Discarded railway sleepers, for example, are of inestimable value in the country, apart from their worth as fuel; and even the 'chairs' come in handy, as the saying is. The latter, when attached to a wire or rope in rigging-stane fashion, are excellent for weighting thatch or a roof of slatted felt. And they can be used conveniently as anchors for small craft, or as weights for fishing-nets.

A country upbringing, moreover, tends to make one observant, though perhaps also a little inquisitive. Despite modern improvements in transport and the introduction into the countryside of so many of the amenities of the town, the stranger passing through a Highland village still excites curiosity. Who can he be? the villagers ask. What brings him this way? Where can he be going? Should an unknown car trundle by, or even an unknown cyclist, country folk will hurry to door or window to have a look. If they discern no outward sign enabling them to say who passes, where he is passing to, and why he passes, they guess and guess. I have relatives in the Hebrides, who never fail to ascertain by nightfall everything that is to be known about a stranger who may have gone by earlier in the day.

Not so with the towns. One seldom has much truck with one's next-door neighbours. Certainly in Edinburgh one would not as much as know their names, were it not that its citizens rather specialise in brass name-plates, conspicuously displayed. But for the fact that the Colonel was never quite able to rid himself of the natural inquisitiveness of the Stornoway people, we would have known a great deal less about the affairs of our friends and acquaintances! He had an astonishing knack of getting people to unburden their minds to him, and to tell him private particulars about their lives and the lives of those more closely associated with them. From people he met quite casually, he had the flair for extracting the most intimate details of their existence. As an octogenarian, he walked each forenoon to a certain seat on the Bruntsfield Links, at Edinburgh. There he engaged in conversation with all and sundry. When he returned at lunch-time, he used to relate complete family histories to us. When we enquired of him how it came about that his informant had communicated this or that piece of very confidential news, he would reply: "Well, I *asked* him! One never learns anything without some effort!"

The towns, of course, have their corresponding advantages; and towns-people are facile where the country-bred are apt to be clumsy. The former can dodge in and out among traffic in a manner that literally puts the fear of death on country folk. Yet, how many of these traffic-dodgers could cross a swollen stream in darkness by a slippery plank, or find their way among fog-bound lanes?

That the town-dweller should regard dykes and fences as formidable obstacles is quite beyond the comprehension of the countryman. The townsman may be able to leap on to a swiftly moving vehicle with agility and accuracy; but confront him with a paling or a fence, especially one with a strand or two of barbed wire, and he is as helpless as a prisoner in a concentration camp.

* * * * *

There is nothing about the earth so satisfying as ploughing. It would be hard to forget the satisfaction and sense of completion that filled me when, as a child, I ploughed my first furrow in a field at High Wind—the field in the centre of which stands that clump of beeches known as Strachan's Wood. Here, you may remember, General Strachan and his army encamped for a night or two before proceeding northward to Carbisdale, but a few miles away, to engage Montrose in the battle that sealed his fate.

With my feet firmly placed on the sod, my hands on the plough handles, behind a pair of shining horses, and the great, rough hands of the grieve at the inn farm enclosing mine, I started off with a host of seagulls wheeling and crying around me. I was very proud, indeed, of having been a ploughman for those brief, glorious minutes, though you may guess what the furrows might have looked like but for the skilful and brawny arms of the grieve, who must have found my presence something of a hindrance to good husbandry. When, a few years later, Aunt Dorothy harnessed Tommy, our ex-polo pony, to a much smaller plough, in order to till the heathery field in front of the old house at Cnocnamoine, I felt full of confidence. But scarcely had I proceeded a few yards before I realised that Aunt Dorothy's strength and skill were indispensable, if any serious ploughing were to be accomplished at all. For many reasons, ploughing at Cnocnamoine was not too easy. The soil was very thin, very stony, and sometimes very hard. This particular field had not known a ploughshare for nigh a generation. Consequently, tufts of heather, of broom, and of gorse afflicted it sorely. The small plough we had was as much as poor Tommy could have managed at his age. Nevertheless, in assisting with the turning over of those somewhat barren furrows, I felt a complacency peculiarly innermost. It was as if I were breaking in a strip of virgin territory, and contributing thereby even this very small quota to the world's history, since it is the plough, more than any other instrument, that has civilized man, enabling him to transform the wilderness into granaries, the stony places into smiling orchards.

Akin to the spirit of the plough is the gathering of fire-wood in the forest. And few things in life delight me more than the scent of burning wood. Sometimes a whiff reaches one in strange and unlikely places.

Once in Versailles I wandered late among the Petit Trianon Gardens. As I returned home at dusk, the inhabitants, just in from their day's toil, were lighting their evening fires of logs hewn in the vast forests on the outskirts of the city. The houses could be seen but dimly; but firelight glowed upon darkened window-panes. In halting for a moment, I closed my eyes and inhaled deeply. Once more I was among the wood-fires of my Highland childhood. And, oh! it was as an aroma from an irretrievable past, for Aunt Dorothy was now beneath the clods, and the old hearths of Cnocnamoine lay open to the sky.

* * * * *

Closely associated with one's early years in the North were the planting and the lifting of the potato crop. The actual planting in spring was one of the most serious occupations of the year, rivalled in importance only by the lifting in the autumn. I always looked forward with eagerness to the supplementary holidays granted to the children of the parish to enable them to assist the farmers or their crofter parents in the gathering of the potatoes, and in pitting them against the coming of rain and frost in winter. When frost got at the potatoes, it was regarded as a major calamity.

It is curious how the potato, a plant of comparatively recent date in this country, should have arrogated to itself, with so little competition, such an important place in rural economy, especially when we remember the hostility shown by the Highlanders to its introduction. When, about the middle of the eighteenth century, Clan Ranald introduced the potato to Uist, he met with the fiercest opposition. His tenants, summoned to receive instruction in planting potatoes, flatly refused to have anything to do with this innovation. Thereupon, they were committed to prison—so extensive were the proprietor's powers in the days of heritable jurisdiction. Having spent a short time in confinement, they eventually consented to plant these unknown roots, for which they still exhibited the greatest contempt. "The laird might, indeed, order them to plant these foolish roots," one of the tenants observed; "but they would not be forced to *eat* them." With difficulty, Clan Ranald got them to lift the crop in the autumn, and convey it to his gate. Not an inch farther would they bring it.

Not long afterwards, however, they came to their senses and, as an economic historian of the period records, "would have gone to prison rather than *not* plant potatoes." To-day, the potato is a very important article in the dietary of the Highlanders and Hebrideans; and in a normal season the most barren holding can produce a fair crop of this once despised tuber.

What else does one recall of rural activities?

Surely, the rhythmic broadcasting of the grain at sowing-time! How few agriculturalists of the present day could scatter the seed to right and to left of them so deftly as did the sowers of my early years! That art has been superceded by what is termed scientific farming. But at that time no one in the Highlands ever sowed the corn in any other way except, perhaps, on one or two of the very large and up-to-date farms of Moray or of Easter Ross. A cart-load of sacks containing the seed corn came trundling over the black earth, a sack being deposited here and there, at fairly regular intervals, upon the field. The sowing-box was suspended in front of the sower by a leathern band slung round his neck. The seed was then broadcast by brawny arms in slow, deliberate rhythm, as the sower went forth in long, emphatic strides, the harrow following after.

* * * * *

There certainly was a catholicity about the people amongst whom I spent my early years. I had much to do with the good, wholesome commonalty of life—with shepherds and ploughmen, foresters and fishermen, blacksmiths and roadmen, and even the tinkers—in fact, with all that great body of mankind using its hands. I moved among them freely, learning much I have never forgotten. We children pricked up our ears when they whispered to one another about the shebeens and illicit stills, for which the Highlands were famed until fairly recent times, and for which the remoter parts of the Outer Hebrides still have a reputation. It was one of my ambitions to locate a still among the hills, since many were reputed to be concealed in the more distant parts of our parish, and rewards were often paid by the inland revenue officials to those prepared to divulge their whereabouts. In any case, the MacGregors, from immemorial time, have had a handsome hand in this illegal traffic. Until roughly half a century ago, smuggling and distilling were two of the chief occupations in the Highlands, more especially in such inaccessible parts as the wilds of Sutherland and Ross, and the heathery uplands of Banff. Apropos the last mentioned, an old record describes Tomintoul as a place where " everybody makes whisky, and everybody drinks it." Robert Hamilton Bruce Lockhart tells us that, when his maternal grandfather, James MacGregor, a native of Tomintoul, walked across the hills with his two brothers and sister, in order to start a farm at Cromdale, in Strathspey, he knew everything about whisky that was to be known, and was not long in setting up his own still. When wandering among these remote hills some years ago, I came upon a tiny ruin in a hollow by a stream, which my Highland fancy immediately identified with the illicit trafficking of my MacGregor forbears.

* * * * *

One of the earliest interests we found in the country was that of telling approximate times on sunny days by the opening and closing of certain flowers. This gave us all immense pleasure. We were proud to regard it as much more scientific than the way in which, in company with the other children of the village, we used to blow the down from the head of a seeding dandelion. It was Linnaeus, the Colonel told us, who carried out at Upsala the idea of arranging clusters of different flowers in the order in which they open and shut. Linnaeus's flower-clock, composed very largely of wild blooms, was based on careful observation of the amount of sleep required by various flowers, and the approximate hours at which, on sunny days, they were inclined to waken. Calculation on sunless or wet days was impossible, of course, since so many flowers do not open at all under such conditions, or only very partially. Plants sleep roughly twelve to eighteen hours—so the Colonel informed us, anyhow; and we never had known him to be wrong about anything. Most of them require an average of twelve. It is not possible for us to imitate in this country Linnaeus's flower-clock with any precision, since the opening and closing times of the same species vary so much according to latitude.

One of the earliest flowers to open in our British latitudes is the wild rose. It wakens about 4 a.m. Shall I ever forget the day when my father first told me this, and I stood stockstill by a cluster of wild roses on the fringe of the first woodland of my life, marvelling that those white, delicate blooms had been awake and fully conscious of the daylight, just when I had been sleepiest?

I cannot say that I now remember more than a few of the opening and closing times of flowers, though the Colonel had supplied me with a formidable list, all of which, no doubt, he had culled during his years of extensive reading. The various flaxes, I recall, open between five and six a.m. The willow-herb shakes off the scales of sleep about seven. Tulips, on the other hand, are among the laziest of flowers: they sleep on till about ten, and often are not wholly awake until an hour later. By noon all the flowers, that will open that day, have done so. In the afternoon they begin to close in regular rotation. In the evening, however, others bestir themselves. The campion, for instance, shows signs of life about six p.m.; and the cactus has been known to defer his wakening until ten. It does seem remarkable that in summery weather botanists are able to tabulate the opening and closing times of flowers throughout the entire twenty-four hours. But it seemed even more remarkable to us in those days that one small head could carry all the Colonel's knew!

* * * * *

Inseparable from country ways are country lore about the weather, and country sayings and beliefs and superstitions.

" Don't bring foxgloves in here! " a friend once said to me with some apprehension. " Foxgloves and hawthorn are faery flowers; and the faeries resent mortals' gathering them."

An Australian lady of Scottish parentage, who had heard a certain amount about the superstitions of her ancestors, but could never quite credit them, told me that, when she boarded a pleasure-steamer a year or two ago in the Kyles of Bute—at Tighnabruaich, to be precise—the captain approached her in a very perturbed fashion to tell her that he could not sail until she had discarded the sheaf of foxgloves she was carrying. He knew from experience they would bring ill-luck. With reluctance, and to the immense surprise of some hundreds of Clydeside onlookers, she threw her precious flowers overboard. The steamer then proceeded on its way.

A few days before Christmas, 1939, two friends of mine, who were renting a cottage at Gomshall, had a surprise visit from their landlord. As he entered, he noticed some holly in a vase on the sittingroom mantelpiece. " You shouldn't bring holly into the house before Christmas Day," he said, " for it will bring you bad luck! " This remark, coming from a person so matter-of-fact, merely amused them. Curiously, that evening they received bad news from Sydney. And out went the holly!

* * * * *

And in what do country folk believe more implicitly than in ghosts and faeries?

The settings of my Highland childhood are renowned for both. Faeries were said to haunt our garden at Applecross; and the ghosts of drovers and of lowing herds have been encountered in the Pass of the Cattle.

Faeries still take the substance out of milk on Raasay, the Isle lying between Applecross and Skye—which reminds me of a certain Miss MacLean, a native of Raasay, who included many faeries among her more intimate friends. She used to tell us that she was once engaged to a faery. And no ordinary one, for he was *Clerk* to the Faeries, she assured us.

Our Highland faeries, I soon discovered, had habits and attributes very similar to the Little Folk of Ireland, about whom Mabel used to tell me. They, too, were given to extracting the *toradh*, or substance, from milk.

I know an Irish lady residing in Kensington, who is very knowledgeable about the Kingdom of Faeries. Her family owns Blarney Castle and the celebrated Stone; and she has lived much among the remoter places of Ireland, where it is firmly believed that, when you capture an elf, you may hold him only as long as you can keep your eyes on him. If you turn your glance aside for the fraction of a second, the spell is broken, and he escapes. When living among the Mountains of Kerry as a child, the old folks used to recite to her the following traditional verses:

Oh! as I went out one winter's night,
A Leprechaun I spied,
With scarlet cap and coat of green,
A cruiskeen at his side.

He hammered and sang with tiny voice,
And drank his mountain-dew:
Oh! I laughed to think he was caught at last;
But the Faery was laughing too.

With eager grasp I caught the elf——
"Your faery purse!" I cried.
"I've given it away," he said,
"To the lady at your side."

I turned to look—the elf was gone;
And what was I to do?
Oh! I laughed to think of the fool I'd been;
And the Faery was laughing too.

CHAPTER XIV

MUSIC IN THE HOME

APART FROM such popular Highland airs as were then on the lips of everyone around us, many of them Jacobite in origin and sentiment, apart also from the few Irish melodies such as *The Minstrel Boy* and *The Wearing o' the Green* that have established themselves so firmly in the North, one did not have much opportunity in those pre-radio days of hearing good music in the Highlands. In this regard, however, I certainly was fortunate in having a musical mother, who loved her piano, and did so much to inculcate in me a proper understanding and appreciation of music. I must have been quite small when she first arrested my attention with Chopin's *Ballade in F Major*. This, I think, was the earliest piece of *real* music I ever heard. It thrilled me utterly, and implanted a love for Chopin which has deepened with the years. Chopin's music so haunted me that it moved me to tears, just as the music of Bach moved the infant Chopin. So sensitive is it, so exquisitely painful, that at times I scarcely can bear it. And, yet, I should prefer to have it to bear than not hear it any more.

I am reminded of a sunny afternoon, in June, in our drawingroom at High Wind, where Mabel sat at her piano, playing through Chopin's *Preludes*. At one time or another, I have listened to many of the world's most celebrated pianists, and even include a few of them among my more intimate friends; but never have I heard any of them play Chopin's *Preludes* as wistfully as did Mabel that afternoon, in the sorrowful days of her marriage and of my childhood. And the one that has lingered in my inward ear since then is that I now know to be the fourth—*Largo in E Minor*. There was sorrow in her playing, that sunny afternoon, as

I, though still so young, well realised, though I could not have appreciated how very unhappy two people, who once vowed they loved, could possibly make one another. The drawingroom blinds were drawn, I remember; and the house was hushed, and scented with sweetpeas and roses from our garden. The rose-bowl on the piano itself, so heavy with soft, velvety petals, I still see clearly in my mind's eye. All those lovely petals have fallen and withered long since, and in more senses than one.

Mabel taught me how to sing. My training began with the more familiar Plantation Songs—'*Way down upon the Swanee River*, *Poor Old Joe*, and the like. Oh! how sad and beautiful I thought them. From that time, I believe, dates my sympathy with the coloured members of mankind. I had been told something in my tender, inarticulate years of the slaves on the cotton plantations. I think I can say without exaggeration that, since the age of three, when Mabel first introduced me to these Plantation Songs, I have been prone to regard the white man as the black man's burden.

The next stage in my musical education was the learning of such traditional songs as *Robin Adair* and *Ye Banks and Braes o' Bonnie Doon* well enough to sing them at local concerts, with Mabel as accompanist. Incidentally, I never appreciated how perfect, musically, are the airs of many of our Scots songs until recently, when a distinguished pianist friend, living within earshot of me in Chelsea, sat down casually at her piano in twilight, and played *Ye Banks and Braes* with an improvised harmony. I doubt whether there is anything finer or more tuneful in the whole of Beethoven or of Schubert than this old, Scots melody.

By the time I was seven, I could perform tolerably well in public. My ear was so perfect that, with the most superficial knowledge of theory, I could render solos, and undertake at a moment's notice to sing alto on any platform, so long as Mabel presided at the piano. She was incapable of striking a discord, which even at that early age meant everything to me. Sometimes she and I went by train to give a musical performance. And what an adventure was the occasion on which we travelled so far as to necessitate our staying overnight in a hotel! Once I sang for half an evening at a concert held in the drill-hall of the Sutherland village of Bonar-Bridge. But I recall more clearly the rest of the programme, which was devoted to ditties of the Harry Lauder variety. These were rendered exclusively by a local tradesman, dressed up in grotesque costume, and twirling an old umbrella. To vociferous encores, he always responded with *Will ye stop yer ticklin', Jock?* Of this neither he nor the audience ever tired.

Will ye stop yer ticklin', Jock?
Oh! stop yer ticklin', Jock!
Dinna mak' me laugh sae hearty,
Or ye'll mak' me choke!
Oh! I wish ye'd stop yer nonsense——
Just look at a' the folk!
Will ye stop yer ticklin'——
Tickle-ickle-ickle-in'?
Stop yer ticklin', Jock!

His other great success had a refrain which we all thought very funny indeed at the time:

Sandy! Sandy! you are a don!
Sandy! Sandy! gi'e us a shake o' yer haun:
A' the lads aboot the toon began to shout and ball
'Hullo, MacTavish! Is yer knees no' cauld?'

For months thereafter every youth for miles around was singing this choice fragment.

But I remember even more vividly than his umbrella and his songs how, in preparing the stage for one of his turns, he slipped on the short steps leading up to the platform, while carrying a tray of dishes. Oh! the clatter of scattering crockery! It was grand! Never before had I witnessed so much destruction at the same heavenly moment. For me this impromptu act was the high-light of the entertainment.

* * * * *

In the Highlands at this time, really good music was rare,

though elsewhere in Britain it was a most melodious era. The Highlanders, of course, are not a musical people in anything but the most primitive sense, despite their claim to the contrary. Many of our Gaelic folk-songs are quite lovely. But it has been left largely to non-Gaels like Sir Harold Boulton, Sir Hugh Roberton, and Marjory Kennedy-Fraser to bequeath them to the world as music, and largely to non-Gaels, also, to interpret them. This statement, I am aware, may give offence, for the Highlanders are particularly touchy when the slightest criticism is made of them. Yet, no one familiar with the average Highlander can deny that he is musically ignorant, and, as a rule, incapable of appreciating good music. He has little conception of what constitutes music, either in the matter of form or of production. That this is so is proved by the performances of our best known Gaelic songsters, and of those who are awarded medals at our annual *Mòd*, or Eisteddfod. At such Gaelic concerts as are held throughout the winter months in cities like Edinburgh and Glasgow, and even London, I have heard Highland audiences applaud the singer of a Gaelic song for an exhibition that, in any reasonably musical community, would have been taken as burlesque. As for piano accompaniment, most Highlanders scorn it, or are content with a little primitive vamping and strumming—so deep-seated is their contempt for a really musical performance, in which voice and piano are regarded as of equal and supplementary importance—so deep-set are they in the superstition that nothing is half as musical as the unaccompanied human voice. What I have said with regard to their antipathy to piano accompaniment is no exaggeration, as is shown by a recent pronouncement by that wellknown Gael, the late Lady Elspeth Campbell, sister of the Duke of Argyll. When presiding at a concert recently held in Glasgow, she remarked that listening to a Gaelic song sung to a pianoforte accompaniment was like listening to two wireless stations simultaneously!

* * * * *

One of the outstanding recollections of childhood at High Wind is the occasion on which everyone for miles around congregated in the waitingroom of the railway station to hear a phonograph—not a gramophone. This phonograph, if not actually one of the first in existence, was certainly one of the first to find its way into the Highlands. The owner was an artist acquaintance of my parents. Each summer this odd fellow arrived at High Wind to paint. He came from Aberdeen, disporting the kilt, and bringing with him a veritable pantechnicon of those cylindrical records that disappeared as the gramophone superceded the phonograph.

That recital in the waitingroom was the most magical thing I ever heard. All the wonders of theatre-land, of the movies and the talkies, of wireless and television, have seemed just a little less wonderful to me than the mysterious voice that spoke from the crude horn of that phonograph. When its owner went to lodge with Mrs MacKintosh, who kept a wee sweetie-shop in Church Street (and who, to perfection, reared marigolds and apple-ringie in her window-boxes), we made countless journeys in that direction for a ha'penny worth of sweeties, in the hope of hearing, and perhaps even *seeing*, this amazing instrument. Mrs MacKintosh's shop was an apartment of her house, on the ground floor, just as one entered; and her lodger occupied a bed-sittingroom opposite. Literally, hundredweights of peppermints and sugary boilings were sold there while he sojourned with his phonograph, since the entire countryside now found occasion to stop, to look, and to listen, in passing this way.

* * * * *

Mabel, I should imagine, was the only person within many miles of our Highland home, who had had a serious musical training, and enjoyed any real knowledge of music. One or two of our neighbours, however, thumped out a few Highland reels, and thought themselves competent musicians. Two people in the parish (or three, if we include the wife of the Auld Kirk minister) played hymn tunes tolerably badly on the harmonium; and some of the crofters scraped away discordantly on their fiddles.

Had it not been for Mabel, I doubt whether the lovely melodies of Franz Lehar, that master among the melody-makers at the time, would have been heard in our parish. Everywhere, except perhaps in the Highlands, the music of Lehar's *Merry Widow* and *Count of Luxembourg* was the vogue. And is there not something imperishable in those melodies of his? Take those introduced into his exquisite operetta, *The Land of Smiles*, for instance. The recent revival of interest in his music, attributable largely to the wireless, must have brought fond memories to many, and certainly to those of us who were young before the War of 1914 made us prematurely old.

In ways, it was a happy time for light and tuneful music—the tail-end of the Edwardian period, and the first year or two of the next reign. Musical comedy was still at its zenith in technique, as well as in melody and harmony. *The Dollar Princess*, *The Chocolate Soldier*, and *The Merry Widow* had burst in upon us, so full of music and colourful pageantry. It was still the age of the waltz—so graceful, so rhythmic, so melodious. But ragtime was already peeping round the corner with *Alexander's Ragtime Band*, threatening to eclipse those lovely melodies of thirty years ago. I often have felt thankful that the family's transference from the Highlands to Edinburgh took place when musical comedy was at the height of its splendour. Otherwise I would have missed much. I certainly would have been denied the opportunity for musical appreciation when most receptive to it. Many, who are perhaps more critical than I, will say that one's sense of musical values is elementary, if one confess to liking Lehar. But what is music for, if it fail to create precisely what Mabel's playing of the *Merry Widow* created in me?

In our home nothing of the *Ta-ra-ra-boom-de-ay* or *Boomps-a-daisy* standard received much encouragement. The nearest we ever got to such banality was when Jessie, badly smitten with *The Perfect Day*, played it from morn till eve,

"... *and is she as beautiful as ever, Alasdair?*"

Mabel, the Author's Mother

The Colonel about 1925, when 77 years of age

commencing long before breakfast, and not desisting until bedtime. The result of this was maddening. Futhermore, it meant that, while this obsession lasted, no one else could get near the piano. The competition between other members of the family to get at the keyboard, solely by way of relieving Jessie of this passion, either by force or by wile, was truly comical. Never before had we been seized with so insatiable a desire to practice our five-finger exercises!

And what was the Colonel's reaction to all this music?

The answer is contained in the plaint to which Mabel was driven at times. "Gaelic for breakfast," she used to sigh, "Gaelic for lunch, Gaelic for tea, Gaelic for dinner, Gaelic for after-dinner; *and always Gaelic airs on the piano!*"

CHAPTER XV

CLAN FEALTY

DURING THE long persecution of the Clan Gregor, culminating in the proscription of the name of MacGregor, under pain of death, there fled from Glen Gyle, at the head of Loch Katrine, a certain Iain MacGregor who, rather than forfeit his name, and surrender those claims which for centuries he and his ancestors had maintained by the ancient ' right of the sword ', now sought refuge among the wild fiords of Western Lewis. My father, a lineal descendant of this fugitive MacGregor, always felt that he had a great deal to live up to. For was not Iain, aforesaid, one of the namely MacGregors of Glen Gyle, that branch of the clan to which the doughty Rob Roy belonged? Rob, indeed, was born in old Glen Gyle House.

For me, as for my father, descent from this fugitive has meant considerable diversity of interest in life. On the one hand, it explains my Hebridean ancestry and, on the other, my filial connection with, and concern for, that portion of the Highlands known as the MacGregor Country. Which is uppermost—my affection for the Isle of Lewis, or for Glen Gyle and that exquisite region in which it lies—I never quite know. In my heart of hearts, Lewis makes the prior claim. When ardent clansmen ask me why, I remind them that more than three hundred years have slipped by since my next-of-kin could claim to have any lineal connection with the MacGregor Country—with Glen Gyle and Loch Katrine and the Trossachs, with Loch Earn, Loch Voil, and Balquhidder. Yet, I like to feel that these two regional interests, both of which have done so much to mould and colour my life, are complementary rather than in any sense conflicting.

Though the Outer Hebrides, and particularly Lewis, a land so tidal of aspect, occupied a unique position in our minds as children, our father never allowed us to forget the land of our MacGregor forbears—a land by contrast so mountainous. Glen Gyle and Loch Katrine occurred in family conversation no less frequently than did Stornoway and Carloway and the sea-creeks and treeless moors of Lewis. As for Glen Gyle itself, father had a vague notion that he ought to have inherited this small but historic property, this ancient patrimony of the MacGregors, now so landless. Short of actually owning it, he felt the best compliment he could pay to past generations of fiery clansmen was to ensure that his children should be familiar with the traditions and achievements of their clan. To this end, therefore, a knowledge of Scott's *Rob Roy* and *The Lady of the Lake* was considered indispensable. Ignorance of these rendered us unworthy of our ancient name. This explains how we all knew, almost by heart, the lengthy Introduction to the former volume. From infancy we had been nurtured on *The Lady of the Lake*, and were conversant with everything of the history and topography of its setting. We knew of Ellen's Isle as soon as we understood that an island is a piece of land entirely surrounded by water. At that time Ellen's Isle was still an isle. We had heard of the Silver Strand before we knew the significance of a silver coin. Although born and bred among mountains and glens, lochs and rivers, none of those physical features was suffered to vie in our imagination with Ben Lomond, Ben Ledi, and Ben Vorlich; with Glen Orchy, Glen Strae, and Glen Lyon; with Loch Lomond, Loch Katrine, and Loch Awe; while the Tummel and the Teith, the Tay and the head-waters of the Forth, were expected to assume in our affection a position not unlike that which Abana and Pharpar had once occupied in the esteem of Naaman, the leper. The very sound of these rivers' names meant more to us than did all the healing waters of Israel, about which we had read so much during those dutiful years of family-worship.

Then, the duel between James Fitz-James and Roderic Dubh provoked our first realisation that men, other than in story-books, engaged one another in mortal combat. The first monster of which we ever heard (apart from '*Himself*', who haunted the old mill at the Milton of Applecross!) inhabited the Goblin's Cave, by the shores of Loch Katrine; and, as for warfare, the manner in which a few MacGregors had routed hundreds, if not *thousands*, of Colquhouns at the Battle of Glen Fruin had been described to us in detail, long before we had even heard of Bannockburn! And there seems to have been no time in our lives when we did not know of Jean MacAlpin's Inn—the celebrated Clachan of Aberfoyle—and of the peeled willow-wand athwart the door, indicating that the premises were occupied. We had also learnt about its elusive minister, the Rev. Robert Kirk, who, after his unwise investigations into the Secret Commonwealth of Elves, Fauns, and Faeries, was spirited away to Faeryland whence, as yet, he has failed to return! Mr Kirk's 'translation' by elfin agency accounted more for my interest in Aberfoyle as a boy than did its associations with the Clan Gregor, though I dared not make such a confession in father's hearing!

As for braes, there were none in the whole world as renowned and romantic as the Braes of Balquhidder, where our father hoped to be buried one day, beside Rob Roy and his kindred, and where, in point of fact, he now lies.

When it came to the Pass of the Kine, however, I experienced difficulty, despite a wellfound reverence for the writings of the Wizard, in envisaging in the Trossachs anything of its kind as breath-taking, as fantastic, as the *Bealach nam Bò*, with which I had become so familiar at Applecross in childhood. The superiority of almost everything else I was prepared to concede.

Of course, the great water-works schemes of the Glasgow Corporation have done much to destroy the beauty of the MacGregor Country, especially where Loch Katrine is concerned. By a succession of Acts of Parliament, more and more of our old heritage at Glen Gyle has been inundated at one end of the loch, while the Silver Strand has vanished at the other. The old home at Glen Gyle is a sorry place at this moment of writing. The City Fathers' vandalism there has been truly terrific.

Nevertheless, we MacGregors always pride ourselves in the idea that we had something to do with the fine water supply of Glasgow—console ourselves, perhaps, with the wishful thought that, had it not been for the Clan Gregor and its patrimony, Glasgow could never have enjoyed anything so excellent. There is romance in every water tap in Glasgow, when you reflect that its content may have laved the shores of Ellen's Isle, and what once was the Silver Strand.

* * * * *

Then there were our clan's relations with the Fiery Cross. Had we not been obliged to commit to memory many of the passages from *The Lady of the Lake* alluding to that ancient method of summoning the clansmen to arms?

When flits this cross from man to man,
Vich-Alpin's summons to his clan,
Burst be the ear that fails to heed!
Palsied the foot that shuns to speed!

One day our father returned from his walk with a large poster tucked under his arm. We all watched him intently, as he unfurled this colourful emblem, and proceeded to affix it with drawing-pins to the study wall, so that, when gazing upon it in pensive mood, he might recall the glowing deeds of his ancestors. Having noticed the poster displayed on the hoarding in the railway station, he obtained a copy from the stationmaster, no doubt adding weight to his request by mentioning that he was the Bard of the Clan Gregor, the first since the resuscitation of the name of MacGregor by special Act of Parliament in 1774! The poster was designed to entice holiday-makers to visit Lochearnhead, in the heart of the MacGregor Country.

It depicted a red MacGregor, wearing a kilt of Rob Roy tartan, a tam-o'-shanter, and deer-skin brogues, tripping lightly through the heather, and bearing aloft a flaming torch typifying Sir Walter Scott's romantic (though quite erroneous) conception of the Fiery Cross. Printed conspicuously across the heather in the foreground were the four lines just quoted. For a year or more, this railway poster retained prime place on the study walls. Against its removal the Colonel had given the strictest injunctions. Even when it became faded and a little tattered, he found it a source of inspiration, and an excuse for dreams.

Besides all this, father certainly expected us to know something of the several Acts of Parliament condemning the Clan Gregor, and ultimately proscribing the very name of MacGregor, under pain of death. It was also desired that we should be conversant with a few of the rude and harsh things the Privy Council had said about us from time to time. Were they not written indelibly in its *Register*, which might be consulted at any time on the shelves of the Advocates' Library?

The trials and tribulations of the Clan Gregor, the defeats and failures it had suffered, were as persistent a topic in the home as the familiar panegyric of its valour and successes. So, we knew its wails and woes, its dirges and coronachs, as well as its rallying-songs and battle-cries. To my father's way of thinking, no male songster incapable of rendering *MacGregors' Gathering* had a right to appear on a public platform at all. About those unable to sing our Clan's laments, however, he did not offer the same criticism. These, for some extraordinary reason, we could sing quite satisfactorily ourselves. I believe the first thing my father ever sang to me, while he carried me round the room in his arms as an infant, was an ancient, traditional setting—in the Gaelic, of course—of the *Lament for MacGregor of Roro*. One day, when searching Glen Lyon with my camera, I unexpectedly came upon Roro, which now consists of little more than a farm and a cottage or two. Was this the scene, I asked myself, that had given to the world that lovely lament my old father used to croon to me in my infancy? Every note and syllable of it I still remember; and I was enchanted when, a year or two ago, and quite by accident, I lit upon an unpublished version of it in an old manscript of music, and found how little it differed from the rendering I have known almost all my life.

* * * * *

So deeply had the royalty of the MacGregors been impressed upon us as young children, that we rather looked upon ourselves as God's chosen people. Consequently, we were puzzled by finding no mention of the MacGregors in the Bible! After all father had led us to believe from infancy about our noble race—about our royal heritage—this seemed to us an unwarrantable omission.

Royal? Yes, by all means! Claiming descent from no less illustrious a personage than Kenneth MacAlpin, first King of Scots, we were naturally prone to regard ourselves as being more royal than the King himself! Was not our very motto—*'S Rioghail mo Dhream:* Royal is my Race—incontrovertible evidence of this? Were we not the only clan entitled, by virtue of our royal lineage, to carry the crown on our crest?

"Who, in comparison with the ancient Clan Gregor," the Colonel would ask, "are the Windsors?"

"Mere upstarts!" came the assured reply, since on matters of such import he preferred to answer his own questions, rather than court any hesitancy or contradiction on the part of the listeners.

Was not the *Lia Fail*—the Stone of Destiny, at Westminster—the Coronation Stone upon which our ancestors, the descendants of Kenneth MacAlpin, were crowned for at least five hundred years before the Hammer of the Scots carried it off into England? And, if *that* bore but inadequately the imprint of antiquity, could we not claim that this was the stone upon which Jacob had rested his head at Penuel, and that ever afterwards was carried by the Israelites? The more reason for our astonishment, therefore, that the scribes should have omitted to mention us in Holy Writ!

* * * * *

The prowess of those Mighty Men of Valour who, with David, vanquished the Philistines—the Tachmonite, who sat in the seat, chief among the captains, who lifted up his spear against eight hundred, and slew them all at one time; Eleazer, who smote the Philistines until his hand was weary, and clave unto the sword; Shammah, who stood his ground so nobly, slaying the enemy until he had wrought a victory for the Lord—*their* prowess, *their* valour, was negligible as compared with that of certain MacGregors who, though pursued with fire and sword, and put to the horn at the Cross of Edinburgh, carried the war into the enemy's camp.

Moreover, no athlete in history could have performed so miraculous a feat as did the fleeing MacGregor who gave his name to the celebrated Leap in Glen Lyon! What Holinshed said of the Scots in Elizabeth's reign might have been recorded with particular reference to the Clan Gregor. " Thereunto we find them to be couragious and hardy, offering themselves often unto the uttermost perils with great assurance, so that a man may pronounce nothing to be over harde or past their power to performe."

As for downright strength, Samson would have been a weakling in the grip of Rob Roy!!

With all this eulogising of anything and everything relating to the MacGregors went a corresponding hatred of anything connected with the Clan Campbell. In our home, as in many others in Scotland, even at the present day, anti-Campbell feeling was always maintained at a high pitch of efficiency. We had heard so much about the schemings and treacheries of the Campbells, especially in relation to the downfall and misfortunes of our own kindred, that we never quite felt ourselves able to trust the most innocent classmate of that name! Our father, like so many of our clan with long memories, was as well versed in the misdemeanours of the wretched Campbells as he was in the valorous deeds of the MacGregors. Bruce Lockhart (whose mother, by the way, was a Strathspey MacGregor) tells us of a maternal ancestor of his who, in refuge among the forests of Strathspey after 'The Forty-five', used to while away the time in adapting the metrical psalms to express his anti-Campbell sentiments. One notable effort of his ran as follows:

The Lord's my shield: I shall be stout
With targe and trusty blade:
Though Campbells come in droves about,
I shall not be afraid.

Wholesale denunciation of the Campbells elicited that the MacGregors were by no means the only clan to have suffered grievously at their hands. There were the MacDonalds, the clan which, after our own, always came next in our hearts, partly on account of what they, too, had endured from the Campbells (as witness their fate in Glen Coe), but chiefly, I think, because our maternal grandmother was a MacDonald. We have lots of MacDonald kinsfolk, therefore, as well as a few bearing the names of MacKenzie and MacLeod. But, much as the Colonel encouraged us to maintain a felicitous disposition toward the MacDonalds, MacKenzies, and MacLeods (in case it should turn out that they were distantly related to us), they must not be allowed to usurp in our affections the place assigned to the MacGregors!

Of the achievements of members of our Clan, whether at home or abroad, the Colonel learnt with joy, particularly when they were of a martial character. He regarded them as undeniable proof that 'the Old Name' was rising again from the dead, after a persecution and proscription lasting nearly two and a half centuries. When David MacGregor, an Edinburgh clansman of ours, was awarded the V.C., posthumously, in 1915, the Colonel was speechless with pride and gratitude. In the service of king and country, poor David had gone to his death, and in so doing had added yet another distinction to the emblazoned escutcheon of the Clan Gregor.

Conversely, news that any of the name was in trouble with the police authorities depressed him sorely, since it brought dishonour on the name. Even now I think I hear him, while reading his evening paper, bemoaning the conduct of some obscure labourer named MacGregor, convicted of drunkenness and creating a breach of the peace, and fined forty shillings! The MacGregors, you see, had always been law-abiding and loyal to the crown; and such drunken behaviour tended to give the world a false impression of them!

* * * * *

And to what did all this clan fealty lead?

The answer is that it led to a certain amount of family impoverishment on the one hand (since it meant that father zealously neglected more important matters for it), and to his being elected Honorary Bard to the Clan Gregor, on the other. The latter was a distinction he cherished more than anything else in life. All other things he had accomplished were trivial in comparison. "After all," he used to soliloquise, "*anyone* might have discovered the phenomenon of the Great Mekong River and Lake Telé-sap. *Anyone* might have penetrated into the wilds of Siam and Cambodia. *Anyone* might have been lost for months in the heart of Indo-China. *But only one person in existence could become Bard to the Clan Gregor—Bard to the Clan Alpin of ancient lineage!*"

His election to the bardship of so royal a race—the first, as he used to remind us, since the original proscription, away back in the closing years of the sixteenth century—was to him as a foretaste of paradise itself. The Clan Gregor Society (one of the oldest, if not actually *the* oldest, clan associations in the world) conferred this honour some time after his final return from India, toward the close of Victoria's reign. By his writings in the East, and by his Gaelic songs, he had done much to merit this peculiarly unremunerative distinction. He had toiled assiduously, by word and deed, to restore 'the Old Name' to favour. In fact, he himself felt that no one, except perhaps Sir Walter Scott, had done so much to revive interest in, and concern for, it. "Dead for two and a half centuries," he used to say, "and now rising resplendently from its grave!"

Our father's love for Scott, largely because of what he had done for the MacGregors, was profound. It produced a family bias for everything associated with the word, Waverley. Our railway journeys from Edinburgh in later years had to be made from the *Waverley* Station. The books we were encouraged to read before all others were the *Waverley* Novels. If we spent a night or two in Glasgow, elsewhere than with friends, we invariably put up at that old-fashioned, family establishment known as Cranston's *Waverley* Hotel, in Sauchiehall Street. When a change was desired, we merely went to the *Ivanhoe*, in Buchanan Street, for, although Waverley did not actually occur in its name, it was at least the title of one of the Waverley Novels. Even though at times it would have been more convenient to travel between Edinburgh and Glasgow by the 'Caley' route, we dutifully made for the Waverley Station to entrain on the old North British system for Queen Street, and thence, making our exit by a side passage, reached the door of the Ivanhoe by walking fifty yards or so through an alleyway—Dundas Lane, I think they call it. I have a faint recollection, too, that in those days our sojourn at the Ivanhoe had an additional recommendation in that the proprietor was one of our clansmen. The Colonel believed in patronising members of that august fraternity when possible, even if it amounted to no more than occupying one of the Ivanhoe beds for a night or two!

This obsession even extended to our writing equipment: none but MacNiven & Cameron's famous Waverley pen-nibs ever found favour with *our* household. A Waverley nib transfers to paper these very words in their original form.

They come as a boon and a blessing to men,
The Pickwick, the Owl, and the Waverley Pen.

* * * * *

There is little doubt that father's reverence for the name of MacGregor and for everything pertaining to our clan amounted to a mild form of insanity. Yet, it did much to sustain him in honour throughout life. Fear of eternal punishment would have deterred him less from felony than would the conception that felonious behaviour was unworthy of 'the Old Name'. And we were all brought up in this belief. To lie or to deceive was bad enough in an ordinary person; but that anyone bearing the tried and trusted name of MacGregor should break his bond was so frightful that all the resources of the English language were inadequate to express the enormity of such misconduct. To break one's word, to forego one's pledge, he considered to be the greatest disgrace one could bring upon the time-honoured name. In this connection he always cited the case of MacGregor of Glen Strae, who kept his word although he knew that in so doing he was granting asylum to the murderer of his own son and heir. In fulfilment of his pledge, did he not even escort the fugitive Lamont safely through watch and ward, "far past Clan Alpin's outmost guard," and incidentally provide Scott with the theme for *The Lady of the Lake*?

"Swear by the Grey Stane on Inch Cailleach!" the Colonel would command, when disciplining us in matters of truthfulness and honour. This ancient emblem of the MacGregors meant much more to him than did the historic Black Stone of Iona, upon which the most sacred and binding oaths were taken in olden times.

One day he took me, as on a pilgrimage, to see the Grey Stane. We travelled Loch Lomond by steamer from Balloch to Balmaha. There we disembarked, and, hiring a rowing-boat, ferried ourselves across to Inch Cailleach, the Isle of the Old Women—the Nuns. Through long grass we went, following a path among dense and hoary woodlands.

And there, sure enough, in a clearing just by the gate of an old MacGregor burial-place, in the heart of the Isle, was the Grey Stane itself. The occasion was one of great interest to us both; but I could see from my father's demeanour that, for him, it was also a solemn moment.

"Haven't I enjoined you all your life to do no mean thing, such as might discredit 'the Old Name'? There, Alasdair, in very truth, is the Grey Stane, by which I so often have asked you to give your word of honour!"

To this day the dead in that sequestered corner of Stirlingshire around Balmaha—Buchanan it is called—are ferried across that narrow stretch of Loch Lomond to the burial-ground by the Grey Stane on Inch Cailleach.

CHAPTER XVI

SOUTHWARD TO EDINBURGH

City of mist and rain and blown grey spaces,
Dashed with wild wet colour, and gleam of tears.

I OFTEN RECALL these lines with which Alfred Noyes begins a poem of his on Edinburgh, especially when ruminating on that city as I have known her since I first went to school there. The joy with which I set foot in Edinburgh was overwhelming, exceeded only by the delight derived from my first weeks there, seeing much in an environment so novel, and yet so austere. Our father had brought the family south early in September, that it might get acclimatised, as it were, before the commencement, on the first Tuesday in October, of the session at the Merchant Company Schools—at George Watson's Boys' College for his sons, at George Watson's Ladies' College for his daughters. The process of acclimatisation was spent very agreeably during those first mellow weeks in the Scottish Capital.

Of Edinburgh we already had heard a certain amount. The name had occurred in the history lesson at Inverness on innumerable occasions; and we often had listened to the Colonel as he told himself audibly how important it was that the family should quit the Highlands for the educational amenities of this great and historic city. And had not Aunt Dorothy spoken to us repeatedly of Auld Reekie? So, one memorable morning we said farewell to Inverness, and set out on the longest train journey hitherto experienced. We were enchanted with everything to be seen from the carriage windows, enthralled by all the odds and ends the Colonel was able to tell us of this place and that, as the train hurried us southward to our new abode. What thrilled us more than his explaining that the green stretches of disused road, glimpses of which we got about Dalwhinnie, were parts of General Wade's old military road, constructed, as were so many others by him, for the pacification of the Highlands after 'The Forty-five'? Little did I think then that a time would come when, for sheer pleasure, I would follow Wade's roads on foot, for miles and miles, through this wild and wonderful country! When I find myself at Dalwhinnie, I scarcely can resist the temptation to tarry for a day or two in the neighbourhood, searching out all these old military routes with my camera, and thereafter, perhaps, striking westward over the Corrieyarrick and down into the Great Glen at Fort Augustus.

On this railway journey the name of every station had to be noted, whether the train drew up at it or not; and our precocious Iain was very elated at his having observed the height attained by the line where, in traversing the only break in the Grampian chain hereabouts, it reaches the summit of the mountain-pass known as Drumuachdar. How often since that first journey between the Highlands and Edinburgh has my eye caught sight of those boards, standing in heather but a stone's-throw from the line, denoting the point at which the railway climbs to an altitude of 1,484 feet above sea-level! Though I must have travelled through Drumuachdar hundreds of times in the intervening years, by rail and by road, awheel and afoot, I still regard those boards, one on each side of the line, with the same childish wonderment as on the first occasion I saw them. There is a romantic touch about them, and perhaps even a quiet air of defiance, drowsing there in Highland summers of heather-scent and bee-hum, on the boundary between the shires of Inverness and Perth, weathering there in Highland winters of black rains and snowstorms, proclaiming with such constancy to all who may journey this way that the long strain of ascent is accomplished, and the jolly rattling and bucketing of swift descent is about to begin—down to the wee station at Dalnaspidal, to the south, or to Dalwhinnie, to the north. " What if it should come off the rails? " I asked myself in later years, on lowering the carriage window to witness the more vividly this reckless spectacle. When, in an endeavour to make up lost time (since all sorts of happenings delayed our Highland trains, especially in winter), excessive speed was resorted to in running downhill toward Dalnaspidal, I used to wonder whether we could avoid over-shooting the station. This familiarity with trains inspired in me the desire to be an engine-driver when I grew up. It also explained the surprise with which I first saw a traction-engine, prowling loose along the road passing through High Wind. Earlier that day, it had hauled caravans and merry-go-rounds and swing-boats to a paddock by the roadside, where a travelling circus was erected annually in pre-war years. I thought that great, fuming monster so out-of-place on the highway, when all the engines I had seen hitherto had been confined to long, metal rails that, we had been told, led to Inverness, and thereafter to great and wonderful places like Edinburgh and Glasgow and London! By the time that the roadmenders visited our locality, complete with steam-roller and with bothy on wheels, we were quite accustomed to seeing these strange, rail-less objects puffing along from place to place, though, for the most part, traffic on our Highland highways still consisted of vehicles that were pushed or pulled by man or harnessed beast. Very few motor-cars had travelled as far north at that time, chiefly owing to the unsuitability of the roads.

There is another curious recollection I have of that first big journey southward, namely, the point at which one could detect from the carriage window just where the Highlands and the Lowlands meet. Though, strictly speaking, all Perthshire is a Highland county, on reaching that stretch of the Garry near Blair-Atholl, one begins to realise that the Highlands lie behind, and the Lowlands ahead. The Grampian wilds have now given way to fertile farmlands—to the carselands of a low country, soft of air and mellow in fragrance. Hereabouts the transition is most marked. The heather has been displaced by clover: the rivers run less impetuously: the mountains are less austere: the valleys are broad, and rich in alluvium: the harvests are luscious, and droop with weight. The cottage gardens are no longer devoid of colour. Their phloxes and rambler-roses are drowsy with the hum of bees; and the atmosphere is tinged with warmth and tranquillity.

* * * * *

By the time we reached Edinburgh, we were as children hypnotised—dazed with revelry, as it were. The train had actually taken us through the Pass of Killiecrankie, where, in 1689, as we had been taught at Inverness, that notorious enemy of the Covenanters, John Graham of Claverhouse—"Bonnie Dundee"—had fallen in the battle in which the Highlanders, under his command, had routed King William's troops. At Killiecrankie we had gone through our first railway tunnel, and were thrilled at the prospect of more to come—the tunnel at Dunkeld, for example, or the two at Glenfarg and at Inverkeithing. And (what was more gratifying than anything) we now could say that we had seen the Forth Bridge with our very own eyes, and had travelled over it! If Edinburgh could provide us with sights and experiences so breath-taking as those we had enjoyed on this first journey from the Highlands, we certainly were in for a grand time.

EPILOGUE

Applecross Revisited

THE AUTUMN of 1939 found me in Inverness, having motored up through the Great Glen in a Morris Eight. With a few days in hand and no commitments of any kind, I decided to make a pilgrimage to Applecross. The day was still young as I set out by the shores of the Beauly Firth in mellowing sunshine. On reaching Dingwall, I turned westward by Garve and Auchnasheen. At Lochcarron I wired to Applecross the possibility of my arrival there, later in the day, though by far the more strenuous part of the journey still lay before me, and I was in some doubt as to how the Morris, laden with a fair quantity of luggage, would behave on the climb from Loch Kishorn to the summit of the Pass of the Cattle. I never fully realised how stupendous an ascent this is, until I tackled it that autumn day, and under the most favourable circumstances. Nor do I think that I ever thoroughly appreciated the efficiency of the cheap, modern car, and the performance of which it is capable. Here was dead metal transformed into something vital. That long, steep climb certainly impressed upon me how isolated we were at Applecross from the viewpoint of overland communication. It seemed incredible that in childhood, and at a time when no motor vehicle in existence could have managed the first hairpin bend, I so often had travelled with my parents over this very mountain-pass in a pony-drawn trap. Little wonder, I reflected, that in my tender years I used to clamour to alight, that in so doing I might subtract from the pony's load at least my own weight of two or three stone!

Having attained the summit, I drew up for a few minutes

and stepped out with a sense of achievement and of infinite wonderment. The climb had been a thrilling experience. I dared not relax speed for one moment until the highest altitude had been attained, since the steepness of the gradient and the stark formidability of everything around made it evident that a second's slackening, a second's hesitancy, would have frustrated any endeavour to reach my destination. Considered in terms of transport, Applecross is still very much in the heroic age.

Although the clouds hung low, and a chill pall of mist hid some of the finest mountain scenery in the land, that rock-strewn mountain-top, retreat of the ptarmigan, cast an eerie spell over me. It now seemed unreasonable—nay, ungracious—to be in too great a hurry to descend. So I lingered awhile in this weird wilderness of stone, picking ripe blaeberries among such sparse vegetation as its crevices could support. It was surprising to find this tiny, wild fruit so plentiful at such an altitude, and in surroundings so barren and sterile. Under a transient lane in the mist stretched a long, narrow strip of silvery sea, terminating at the base of very distant hills, half in varying shades, and half in brilliant sungleam—a peep of the Outer Hebrides in very miniature, the golden shafts of an obscured sun thrust down through storm-clouds, tinting these faraway hills with the blues and greens of peacock. A luminous glimpse of the haunted hills of Harris, to be sure—the fleeting lustre of Elf-land.

Men give to this desert of rock the name of Applecross Forest. But, like so many similar regions in Scotland, there is precious little about it to suggest a forest in the accepted meaning of that word, except, maybe, where one finds the stumps and roots of trees buried aeons ago, and now protruding here and there among the peat-hags. It is a forest only in the sense that it is a *deer* forest: deer live and move about it in great numbers, and are slain there for pleasure. In time of severity, the traveller in these parts may even come upon a herd of deer lying upon the snow, dead from starvation. There is never too much sustenance for beast at any time among these wilds. When they become one vast snow-field, there is none at all; and the deer, sometimes dilatory about descending to lower altitudes, simply lie down on the snows to die. Thus, in course of time, when the snows have vanished from all but the sunless pockets of the hills, the wanderer in such country may find little heaps of bleached bones in close proximity to one another. And, if he know anything of the ways of deer, and of the struggle they have to survive a severe and prolonged winter in such inhospitable surroundings, he may visualise how these bones came to lie there.

Deer perish in this way all over Scotland. A few years ago, a friend of mine, in descending one of the snow-fields of the Cairngorms, suddenly found himself confronted with a herd of a dozen or more, lying motionless on the snows below him. At first he could not understand why, on his coming so close to them, they did not rise and run. He found they were dead. They had stayed up too long.

* * * * *

By tea-time I was descending the seaward side of the Pass; and it was early evening before I reached Applecross. About my arrival there was an element of homecoming. As I passed along 'The Street', the villagers were all in their doorways, or seated on the sea-wall in front of their homes, curious to gaze at the fellow so many of them had known as a little boy. Most of the older inhabitants were gone—the MacRaes at the inn, for example, and Sandy, and the Dupple. But there still were many who remembered me, and who smiled shyly as I made my way to the house of Murdo MacRae, the ferryman. By the gable of this house stood Mary, his wife, waiting to welcome me. "And did you notice all the folk out to see you come past?" Mary asked me. "I did that!" I replied, well aware that my telegram would have occasioned something of a mild sensation. This may appear conceited and boastful to the southron, unfamiliar with all that a Highland homecoming implies, after an absence of many years. I mention it merely to illustrate how an isolated community cherishes the return of someone it has once loved.

A few moments later I was seated by Mary MacRae's fireside, about to partake of that hospitality so characteristic of the Western Highlands and the Hebrides. The kettle was boiling in anticipation of my arrival; and, while Mary dished the meal, I sped out to the cliff of my childhood, but a stone's-throw away, just by the sea-gate of our old garden. There I sang out to the sea and the Isles of Raasay and Skye. Echo answered me back, as of yore. But his answering brought a secret sob, for my old and belovéd father had gone, and these wild hills and seas knew him no more. Had Murdo MacRae not been following closely in my footsteps, I assuredly would have wept at the passing of my father, and at the incomparable beauty of the setting of my childhood. The quiet simplicity of everything was a peculiar reminder that I had come back to the old and elementary world I had deserted for the will-o'-the-wisps of a civilization so far removed from the fundamentals of land and sea and sky, and from God's pure air—a civilization polluted with soot and fumes, disturbed by the roar of wheels, and liable at any moment to be laid waste by screaming bombs. Not a murmur came from the sea this tranquil evening. Everything had taken on an air of strange quietude. Quack of mallard out over the bay, honk of a skein of wild geese travelling in arrow-head formation between Skye and the lone lochs high up among the hills behind us, and the intermittent *cág-cág-cág* of the black-backed gull—the weirdest of cries—were all that could be heard. Of human activity there was no sound.

As there was still a certain amount of daylight left when we had finished our meal, I went out to investigate some of the more accessible of my early haunts. All things within easy reach appeared so small and compact: distances I had thought quite considerable had shrunk to a few yards. Nothing but the mountains maintained their magnitude.

Near at hand stood the old mill, its rotting exterior covered for the most part with weed and moss, its cobwebbed interior no longer the abode of the Diabolical One. It had not done a wheel's turn for years; and old Mr Matheson had gone to his rest. Behind was the loch, strewn with water-lilies as in the autumns of my first, faint recollections. By its fringe I searched for Johann Finlayson's cottage, but it had gone. The merest rickle of stones, half hidden among grass and bog-myrtle, indicated where it once stood. The old woman had passed on, long ago; and of Johann the villagers could tell me nothing.

The older inhabitants were anxious to speak with me of my people. In solemn whispers, they asked me about my mother, in whom they apparently had maintained a life-long interest almost unique in its suggestion of reverence. This I thought curious at the time, especially as I was more anxious to speak with them of the Colonel—more anxious for reminiscences of the dead than of the living.

" And where's your mother, Alasdair? Dare we ask if she's living still? You know, we all say yet that she was the most beautiful leddy we had ever seen. There's never been the like of her in Applecross since the day you all went away and left us here. . . . And is she as beautiful as ever, Alasdair? "

The natives' recollections of Mabel and of her beneficence touched me deeply. They were like the stories of a faery princess of exceeding beauty, who had come into their midst to minister to their needs, and to comfort them in sickness. They spoke of her as of someone more akin to the world of the spirit than to the world of the body. To the Colonel, on the other hand, they referred more freely, and with a touch of jocularity. He remains in their memories as a real person, a human being of flesh and blood, a mortal capable of being overtaken by the death that brings us all into the category of mortals. But not so with Mabel. She lives in their hearts as a visitor from Faeryland.

News of Mabel's loveliness and charm had travelled far. One day recently, in the house of a friend in London, I met a learned and elderly Scot who, for a great number of years, had been engaged in missionary work in China. He straightway proceeded to tell me that, although he had never seen my mother, he had heard tell of her exceeding beauty, even in China. Friends of his used to remark that never in their lives had they seen anything quite as perfect as the picture of Mabel at High Wind, moving leisurely among the flower-beds in her garden, the sun-gleam on her golden hair—" just like a flower herself, " they always added.

* * * * *

Even the postman's importance has waned to some extent in this outlandish place. In this connection, one is reminded of an old postwoman in Easter Ross, whom the local people called Eppack-Steppack, and who was bemoaning the decline in the popularity of those engaged in delivering the mails in the Highlands. " There was a day," she said, " when I brought the news to everyone in the glen; and they all looked forward to seeing me. Now the wireless gives them the news before I arrive; and they don't mind very much whether I come or not! "

" We're not so isolated as we were in *your* time, Alasdair! " Murdo MacRae observed, on lighting his pipe with a twist of paper, at the commencement of an interchange of reminiscences that carried us well into the night. " The wireless keeps us in touch with what's going on in the outside world; and the old means of communication aren't looked on now with the same reverence. But it's bad enough in winter even yet."

" And do you mind the boat I made for you? " Murdo enquired. " My word, but I had a job with the Colonel over that! I was just beginning to try my hand at the models then. There was no toy-shop nearer than Dingwall. So he got myself to make a boat for you. But I would be giving him all the excuses I could be thinking on. I was busy at the joinery at the time, you see, building houses and the like, and making big boats for the fishermen. And so I couldn't spare the time. Well, I was making all the excuses in the world; and at last I told the Colonel I had no suitable wood."

" Where do you get your wood from? ' says he."

" ' From a wood-merchant in Montrose,' says I."

" Well, he wrote to Montrose; and a suitable bit came by the post. There was no excuse about it then. And that's the way you got the boat you lost yon day in the squall."

At the Highland Villages Exhibition held in Kyle in the autumn of 1939, Murdo MacRae was awarded a prize for a model ship in a bottle. " I'm going on at the models yet," he told me. " I made one in a bottle the other day—a full-rigged ship—sails and all! Ah! I didn't finish at the models yet."

When finally we retired, it was not for long, since Murdo had to be abroad again in two hours' time with his fellow-oarsman, when the mail-steamer was due in Applecross Bay on her return trip from the Outer Hebrides, and they had to attend her with the ferryboat. Except in the most boisterous weather, Murdo MacRae and Murdo Gillanders have ferried out to that steamer, or to her predecessor, twice in twenty-four hours, six days of the week, for fifty years. Very rarely during that incredible period have they taken a few days' holiday; and never have both of them been away at the same time.

The crackling of wood in the kitchen below my attic bedroom awoke me betimes, as Mary kindled the fire in the small hours. And I could hear the phlup-phlup of boiling water poured from kettle to teapot, as she infused a strong brew for Murdo; the disjointed conversation between them in the Gaelic, as he moved between kitchen and bed-closet in his sea-boots; his slow, heavy footfall on the creaking staircase, as he ascended to discover whether I wanted to accompany him and his companion in oars on their early morning pull to the mail-steamer. In a few moments I, too, was abroad; and by 3 a.m. we were leaving for the jetty, a hundred yards or so off, carrying a storm-lantern to light us on our way. Murdo Gillanders was already there with a second lantern. We all talked long in the shadowy darkness of rippling water, until the siren of the steamer, still unseen, signalled the time for our pushing off. We were well out in the bay, resting literally on our ponderous oars, when at last she came in sight, and bore down upon us, guided in our direction by the light of one of the lanterns placed at the bow. On the jetty behind us gleamed the other lantern, left there to guide us back in the dark.

* * * * *

My pilgrimage to Applecross—my sojourn in this Arcadia—revived many of my earliest remembrances.

A whiff from the wood-fires in the village recalled the sizzling of the birch log on the rosy fires of our old home at the Milton of Applecross, when I used to imagine that, perhaps, this sizzling was the chirping of the tiny birds who had inhabited the trees in the leafy months. By the fireside sat my father, quietly engrossed in his reading, soft lamp-glow cast upon the open book. In the chimney a wintry wind made queer noises, sending down little gusts now and then—gusts bringing with them curious wisps of smoke that drifted toward the reading-lamp and, in encircling it, evaporated in some way that I thought quite magical, quite miraculous. Those curly wisps I still smell in imagination, since the fragrance of the wood-fire lingers, when childhood years are gone beyond recall.

I wandered along the shore-road to the old kirkyard and the cell and grave of Saint Maelrubha. There, in the mossy mools, lay so many of the older folks I used to know, their names engraved in lichened stone. Memory and the spell of Maelrubha held me in thrall. Aware that men travelling to war from this Gaelic land, or to far countries, are wont to take with them a handful of this consecrated mother-earth, I too lifted a puckle, that it might also sian *me* in my voluntary exile.

In pausing by the stream still meeting the sea at this point, as in the days of Maelrubha and his monks, I asked myself whether I could be content in the midst of such loveliness and remoteness—such simplicity and loving-kindness—and allow the great world beyond to go turning as it cared. And I found that I could not, for, although much had remained as I had left it, the village I had known in childhood had all but fled, and the bay was as a place of vanished waters.

INDEX

PRINTED IN GREAT BRITAIN BY
JAS. TRUSCOTT & SON LTD.,
LONDON & TONBRIDGE.